Vocal Power

Vocal Power
Harnessing the Power Within
The Vocal Awareness Method

Arthur Samuel Joseph

Vocal Awareness Institute
P.O. Box 261021
Encino, CA 91426-1021

Vocal Awareness Institute
P.O. Box 261021
Encino, CA 91426-1021

Book design by Jenn Ramsey
Editorial supervision by Chad Edwards

The author of this book does not dispense medical advice or prescribe the use of any techniques as forms of treatment for physical or medical problems without the advice of a physician, either directly or indirectly. The intent of the author is only to offer information of a general nature to help you in your quest for emotional and spiritual well-being. In the event you use any of the information in this book for yourself, which is your constitutional right, the author and the publisher assume no responsibility for your actions.

Library of Congress Cataloging-in-Publication Data
Joseph, Arthur.
    Vocal power : harnessing the power within / by Arthur Samuel Joseph.
        p. cm.
    Includes bibliographical references and index.
    ISBN 1-58872-064-0
        1. Voice culture. I. Title.

PN4162.J67 2002
808.5 dc21

                                                                2002034110

06 05 04 03   4 3 2 1
First printing, October 2003
Printed in the United States of America

Endorsements

"It's been 25 years of trust and growth
with Arthur and his Vocal Power techniques.
These are simple tools that really work."

Lucie Arnaz
ACTRESS, SINGER, AUTHOR

"Arthur Joseph eloquently expresses the
magic alchemy of the voice and provides
the reader with the tools to tap into its power,
thus releasing the infinite possibilities
that exist within all of us."

Peter Guber, Chairman
MANDALAY ENTERTAINMENT GROUP

"Arthur's Vocal Awareness techniques continue
to help enhance my vocal stature. The orderly
step-by-step exercises give me usable tools to repeatedly
grow in voice, color, clarity, range, and power."

Arnold Schwarzenegger
ACTOR, ENTREPRENEUR, POLITICIAN

"I was able to learn an incredible amount about my voice and about how to have great impact with more pleasure and less pain."

Tony Robbins
AUTHOR, *UNLIMITED POWER*

"They always say that what comes out of your mouth is who you are. . .well, Arthur is going to make it sound great and make it mean something."

Pat Riley
NBA COACH

" . . . Arthur Joseph's proven techniques will make your voice heard and get you where you want to go."

Jack Canfield
COAUTHOR, NEW YORK TIMES BESTSELLING
CHICKEN SOUP FOR THE SOUL SERIES

"More than any other teacher, Arthur's work has profoundly impacted my life personally and professionally. Together we found my real voice and a more authentic me. I so believe in his work that I bring him to Dream University to teach my students."

Marcia Wieder
"AMERICA'S DREAM COACH"

"Arthur makes you focus on the important things you might not take the time to do."

Bob Calderoni, President and CEO
ARIBA, INC.

"Arthur Joseph is a master teacher in the process of communication. My skills as a businessman, lawyer, and community activist are greatly enhanced by his collaboration, his care, and his teaching."

Matt Fong
FORMER CALIFORNIA STATE TREASURER

"The Vocal Power work that Arthur does and the insights he shares are profound, inspiring and deeply spiritual. My own life has been transformed by his unique gift and anyone fortunate enough to learn from him will never be the same."

Rabbi Steven Carr Reuben, Ph.D.

"Arthur Joseph is a friend, teacher, coach, and mentor. His new book, *Vocal Power,* is an extension of his own remarkable prowess as a master enabler. His previous book, *The Sound of the Soul,* changed my life.
Vocal Power: Harnessing the Power Within captures Arthur's passionate belief that vocal awareness can change not only a life-it can change the world."

Michael C. Blackwell, President
BAPTIST CHILDREN'S HOMES OF NORTH CAROLINA,
THOMASVILLE, NORTH CAROLINA

For my family, Rebecca/Isaac/Eli,
without whom life as I know it
would not exist

For my students,
without whose canvas to paint upon
Vocal Awareness would not exist

For my late mother, Betty, my hero,
without her courage and vision
I would not exist

Contents

Foreword

I have spent the better part of my life paying attention to my outward appearance. Being in the spotlight of the sports and entertainment world, I have always been focused on my body image, clothing, jewelry, homes—all the material things of life. I thought that these were the things that formed people's first impressions about me, and I believed that these were the things that would make me happy.

Through my relationship with Arthur Joseph, I have come to learn that the essence of a person comes from within, and that others derive their first impressions, more from a person's voice and inner-emotions, than from the surface characteristics. Arthur's Vocal Power method has been the catalyst to helping me discover that true happiness comes from self-awareness. He has also taught me that the way to improve myself is to focus on my inner strengths and my inner voice.

Michael Irvin
FORMER DALLAS COWBOYS ALL-PRO,
NFL STUDIO ANALYST

Acknowledgments

M any thanks to Stephanie Gunning, whose dedication and ability have helped me immensely in
translating my teaching to these pages. To Debbie
Luican, Mark Misiano, Ira Streitfeld, Chad Edwards,
Charles McStravick, Jill McIntyre, and the rest of the
dedicated Jodere Group for their support and love—
without which this journey could not be taken. And to
Arielle Ford, Brian Hilliard, and Dharma Teamworks
for their belief, vision, and commitment to Source. A
special thank you to Gary Winnick and Lod Cook for
believing in my vision.

Author's Note

The stories in this book are true. However, in an effort to safeguard the privacy of certain individuals who have been my students, some of the names and identifying details of the people mentioned in this book have been changed.

*If you believe in yourself, have dedication
and pride and never quit, you will be a winner.
The price of victory is high, but so are the rewards.*
Paul "Bear" Bryant
FORMER UNIVERSITY OF ALABAMA FOOTBALL COACH

Preface

I'm sure you've heard the expression: "You never get a second chance to make a good first impression." This statement is as true today as it was decades ago—perhaps even more so—as our contemporary lifestyle has become extremely fast-paced. In fact, an opinion is created in three seconds. (Doesn't allow much time for an "icebreaker," does it?) In an effort to be successful and attractive, people spend their time and money on going to the gym; getting the right haircuts; and wearing stylish clothes, makeup, and fashion accessories. But such improvements are external—and they are not enough. If you're not developing your voice—both inner and outer—you're missing the true secret of success.

Have you ever noticed that there are very few successful people with bad voices? Think about it. Except for actress Fran Drescher, the lead in the hit TV show *The Nanny* who turned her dreadful, nasal voice into an asset, most truly successful people have found a way to use their voices to their advantage. Career-wise, improving your voice and accountability greatly enhances your ability to climb the corporate ladder, make big sales, and/or persuade investors to take a risk on your latest project. Today, we also accomplish a huge percentage of our work on the phone rather than in face-to-face meetings. So, vocal technology, such as cellular phones, has clearly impacted the business world. With Internet "chat rooms" (which, ironically, don't involve actual chatting), we're threatened to lose the art of communication altogether. We're becoming depersonalized from our true voices. In addition, developing your voice can vastly improve your rela-tionships with family and friends. It can even help you attract the perfect mate.

Voice is power. Voice is *identity*—how we represent ourselves to the world. As it emerges from the core of our beings, it broadcasts everything about us to the world. Thus, voice is a metaphor, or symbol, of who we are. And since we live in a culture where perception is reality, having a confident, commanding voice and persona can make the difference between being heard and being ignored.

The secret behind the Vocal Awareness method is that it puts you in charge of the body's broadcast system—in charge of the way you are perceived. *Vocal*

Power will teach you how to dictate your identity—as you want it to be—not have it dictated to you. Interestingly, this process of development is not about changing who you are; it's about becoming who *you* are. This is *not* a game—you're really going to *be* it and *show* it.

I believe you already know how to recognize a vocally powerful person. These people have a special presence. They have a remarkable ability to connect with our emotions and draw us into their vision. Not that they always have a "perfect" accent or tone—that's not really the point. But the sound we hear seems congruent to their personality, body, message, and role.

A robust man with a high, breathy voice does not appear congruent, for instance. Remember former heavyweight boxing champion Mike Tyson? His voice does not match the strength of his body. Arnold Schwarzenegger, on the other hand, now enjoys a deep and commanding vocal tone that reflects his powerful body, the action hero characters he portrays as a movie star and his authority as a successful businessman. However, when I coached Arnold, his accent was not the only issue: We also focused on building Vocal Power to enhance his identity by increasing the strength of his vocal muscles, liberating tension, and improving the coordination of his communication. When we first began working together he joked, "My goodness, I didn't know I had a weak muscle in my body!"

Arnold possesses another character trait that people with Vocal Power tend to share, which you will develop by participating in this program: Self-mastery. He is more disciplined and single-mindedly focused than the average person. It made him a great body-building competitor—he was a seven-time Mr. Olympia before becoming an actor—and it helped him reap tremendous benefits from the Vocal Awareness method.

One time I was on a film dubbing stage with Arnold when he taught me a yoga stretch called the "bow" in which you have to stand on one foot and lean forward. We decided to see who could hold the pose longer. I stopped after a minute because I had proved to myself that I could do it. But he held it for several minutes more, just for fun—even though he had already won. As a competitor and in every area of life, he always aims for his personal best. He does this for himself, because it pleases him. He enjoys creating and living a life of excellence.

It is relatively easy to grasp the importance of self-discipline and heightened attention to detail that is essential to excel at a sport, such as weightlifting, or in a performance art, such as dance. And even when they do develop discipline in a sport, most people still don't connect to that discipline in other areas of their lives. Therefore, they never fully integrate or embody their power. A method to develop mastery of the discipline and integrate it thoroughly is now available to all of us. The Vocal Awareness method teaches us a process for creating excellence by working through the medium of the voice.

I originated the Vocal Awareness method almost four decades ago to help people sing, speak, *and be more powerful*. Over the years, it has been enhanced and refined, evolving according to the insights I've gained from working one-on-one and leading group workshops with individuals from every walk of life across the United States, Canada, and countries around the world. I have discovered that this straightforward system benefits all people regardless of their background, what language or regional dialect they speak, and whether they have a formal education.

When I was four, my mother signed me up for accordion lessons. Music has been a part of my life since then. Later, as a teen, I began studying voice. Mrs. Julia Kinsel, my teacher, was like a fairy godmother to me. While others only saw a pudgy, insecure, confused, and lonely 15-year-old, she saw who I really was: a boy with a unique gift. Because she recognized my talent, she allowed me, with her guidance, to conduct my own lessons. She helped me realize that I heard vocal sound differently from other people. I didn't just hear the pitch and the melody of the voice; I instantly felt the emotion within it. It was as though I had "perfect pitch"—though not necessarily to recognize a B-flat when I heard one. Rather, I possess the ability to hear the past, present, and future of a person's life through the vocal sound at a deep emotional level. This rare gift was coupled with an intense desire to understand exactly how sound was made and how to keep improving it technically. Mrs. Kinsel's wisdom, patience, strength, and freedom from dogma liberated me. She opened a door that has since never been closed.

In college I majored in music, philosophy, and psychology. While there, I became a professional entertainer. By age 18, I'd earned my Equity and AFTRA (American Federation of Television and Radio Artists) union cards and was performing in musical theatre, on television, and in nightclubs. I was a member of a professional musical singing group that recorded the Henry Mancini soundtrack to the film *The Great Race*. But a persistent voice inside me wouldn't be ignored. It kept insisting, "You're going to be a teacher, not just a performer." At 18, I began teaching voice privately part-time.

Teaching in those early years was already exhilarating. When I was teaching, I could sense within myself what the sound should be like and the mechanics for producing the sound—but I didn't understand why. After giving lessons, I'd try to figure out the "why." I read books on voice science, experimented on myself, questioned scientists, attended seminars, and gradually made significant discoveries. I loved helping people experience singing—and I was as successful at it as I was at performing. But in my mind, I was still the pudgy, frightened, lonely boy Mrs. Kinsel had met years earlier.

Magic struck in my senior year of college when I met and fell in love with Rebecca. A year later, we were married, in graduate school, and struggling to keep our financial heads above water. I taught voice, as well as music in Sunday school, performed around town, and did various odd jobs. Our gross income together was only about $300 a month. However, at the age of 26, when we had one child, we had saved to buy our first home and were on the path to fulfilling the American dream. Then, I got fired from my full-time job and things became so bad that we were forced to use food stamps for a while.

The reason I'm sharing these intimate details about the course of my life is that my approach to voice and my approach to life are one and the same. During this period of struggle, I was forced to take a hard look at myself and choose the kind of man I would be. In the naked light of poverty, I recognized that I didn't like the man I had become. I'd been using my wife as a scapegoat, telling myself that she wasn't supporting me emotionally to be a full-time teacher. And this was a lie. Rebecca was there for me 1,000 percent! But whether she had been there for me 1,000 percent or one percent didn't actually matter because *I* hadn't been there for my Self. My insecurities were residuals from my childhood. With this realization, I began taking responsibility for, and ultimately ownership of, my life and my destiny. As a result, Vocal Awareness was born.

I placed an ad offering free introductory lessons in a local newspaper and began to attract students. I also began listening to my inner voice. One day on a drive with my family through one of the many canyons in Los Angeles, I became aware of an interesting structure off to the right. But I whizzed on past. Three miles later, I responded to my inner voice, turned around, and came back to examine a pair of enormous 20-foot high gates (actually taken from the set of the film *Ben Hur*). I parked the car, we got out, and walked through the gates. In that moment I entered a new phase of my life.

The gates and grounds of this property belonged to Will Geer, the noted American actor, and his wife, who ran an outdoor theater together. They'd been looking for a voice teacher, and I began teaching them.

Preface

Through the Geers, I met numerous other actors, singers, and professional performers who became my students. At Will Geer's seventieth birthday party I met Michael Learned, who at that time was portraying the mother on the hit TV series *The Waltons*. I soon became her teacher. At that party, I also met actor Ralph Waite (the father on *The Waltons*) and learned that his theater company was looking for a voice teacher. I picked up the phone and called him—several times, in fact—before we finally set a meeting. Toward the end of the meeting, I sensed my presentation wasn't coming across well. (Once again, I heeded my inner voice.) I said, "Ralph, would you like to try an exercise?" Before I left, we set a date to begin the program. I worked for his company for three years.

Around that time, I began working with the Mark Taper Forum in Los Angeles, one of the country's leading regional theaters. The first production I worked on starred Tyne Daly and Eileen Brennan, who both went on to become dear friends and private students. Many years later, this relationship led me to become a professor of voice in the theater school at the University of Southern California. As you can see from these examples, one thing always leads to another. But they wouldn't have if I hadn't committed to my decision to take responsibility for my life and claim ownership of my destiny. To be and give the best of my

Self possible, I had to have the courage to own my power and to face my fears.

Since the origin of the Vocal Awareness method, I have taught it literally in palaces and on skid row. I have taught at Yale University, George Washington University, the University of Southern California, and at the Esalen Institute. I have taught thousands of individuals: corporate executives; politicians; college students; movie stars, such as Anne Bancroft, Edward James Olmos, Faye Dunaway, Jason Robards, and Sally Field; TV stars, such as Sela Ward, Heather Locklear, and William Conrad; broadcasters; and sports celebrities. I have taught secretaries and CEOs, novice announcers and seasoned anchors, housewives and schoolteachers, therapists and doctors. And they have all known success through the Vocal Awareness method.

Now it's your turn.

Introduction

How to Use This Book

In *Vocal Power*, I am going to show you how to master your voice, enhance your Self, and maximize the potential of your life in only minutes a day. Through the exercises of the Vocal Awareness method, you will discover how to use own your voice, develop power through self-awareness, and integrate it into total mind/body/spirit wellness. You'll empower yourself and discover the unique qualities and strength that reside in your soul. From now on, I invite you to think of yourself as a "professional voice user."

I chose to write this book because it was needed. Books on speech therapy, singing, and speaking are readily available. So, too, are books on how to put your life together; how to put your body together; how to forgive; how to forget; how to live in these stressful, high pressure times—but very few of them are comprehensive enough to affect your deepest core of being. Yet knowing how to change is absurdly simple. It is right in front of you—right inside you.

After delving into the nature of "Vocal Power" in Chapter 1 and "Common Vocal and Communication Challenges" in Chapter 2, I will show you step-by-step how to do a daily vocal workout. The physical exercises include breathing exercises necessary for giving birth to the new you; laryngeal strengthening exercises (vocal body building, so to speak); relaxation exercises, which will reduce the tension of the tongue, jaw, neck, and shoulders; and finally, exercises to create the mind/body/spirit connection and enhance conscious awareness. Spend as little as seven minutes a day on this workout or as much as several hours, depending on the level of your desire and ambition. Vocal Awareness will change your voice and your life, and *you* will be doing the metamorphosing.

Don't be intimidated as you open your voice. Be supportive as you experience and explore new possibilities. Think of it as you would if you were taking a tap dancing class for the first time. You'd expect to be a little awkward, wouldn't you? Opening your voice is just a little more intimate.

Throughout the later chapters, you'll be exploring various activities that complement the vocal workout and help you integrate its lessons in other areas of your life. Individual chapters focus on the importance of body language, physical health, self-esteem, and also—my favorite—singing!

We always approach Vocal Awareness—the mind/body/spirit integration and conscious awareness—through seven basic principles that I call "rituals." When a batter climbs into the batter's box, does he just swing? Of course not! He has a ritual before he climbs in and a separate ritual once he is in the batter's box. Maybe he crosses himself. Maybe he touches the rim of his cap, or uses his bat to tap the dust off his shoes. This isn't going to make him a better player—technically. Similarly, a basketball player standing at the free throw line might have a ritual to dribble the ball twice or to spin it three times. This is not going to enhance the arc of her shot. But, in both cases, the rituals are going to help the players focus and pay better attention.

Over the years, I've worked with many professional athletes: tennis players, basketball players, swimmers, runners, and football players among them. They all have their own rituals, which, mechanically speaking, have nothing to do with their particular sport. Rather, rituals help them leave one reality—that of standing on deck or behind the line—and enter another, where they are fully conscious and engaged in the moment at hand—not the moment five seconds later but *immediately*. For the first time, we're taking what we learned on the playing fields of games and are applying them to the playing fields of life.

The Vocal Awareness rituals are based on physical mechanics and moral philosophy. The key to using them is to "listen deeply" and *Pay Attention* to the details. When reading this book, don't take a single thing for granted—not a comma, not a word, not a phrase, not a thought. (Don't think that I'm being maniacal but rather *mindful*.) In practicing the exercises, be equally sensitive to the details of your physical instrument and your psychological state. *The success of this work, as in life, is mastering the subtleties of your individual experience.* Your connection with your authentic Self and your opportunity for profound change lie in that subtle discovery and subsequent awareness.

Welcome. Because I have taken and continue to take the journey—a path toward the sacred—to Vocal Power, I know how to lead you on this path to the discovery and fulfillment of the greatest and best you possible! Place your hand in mine, and we'll travel together for a while.

Voice
of the Monkey Boy

a parable

This is a parable I wrote a few years ago with a
student, Krysta Tabuchi. I'm using it here to
illustrate the journey of *Vocal Power*.

Long ago, a wood carver named Matsugoro
found himself gazing at The Tall One. Standing
proud and almighty, this tree cast the longest shadow
in the village. Because of its indomitable presence
throughout hundreds of years, it became the hub of
this village. With a sigh, he stared at it everyday
while carting his wares to sell on the streets.

As a child, Matsugoro used to climb every tree
that he set his eyes on—all but The Tall One. He
felt free and fearless. He was so daring that he was
called the "Monkey Boy." He didn't just think
about doing things; he did them. When he reached
the top of each tree, he yelled in a clear and loud
voice allowing his spirit to soar.

Years passed. Adulthood took over and
Matsugoro soon found that being so uninhibited
was frowned upon by his fellow villagers. Family

life and hard work were the expected routine. His own work absorbed most of his time and away he toiled. He turned serious and quiet. His dreams faded and he no longer felt like the Monkey Boy.

But every morning it never failed; The Tall One spoke to him with its silent defiance. He never voiced his dream of climbing it, for he never really said anything at all. Keeping to his usual way, he turned into a man of steady but boring virtue. But deep inside, the voice of the Monkey Boy was gently resonating.

One summer day, he awoke feeling the weight of discontentment sitting heavily on his chest. He knew then that it was time to challenge The Tall One.

The first branch was easy to reach. The second and third seemed more spread apart. His body stretched and his hands strained with each grasp. His muscles shook and burned from exhaustion. Nevertheless, he kept looking up while imagining the almost forgotten taste of victory.

The sun grew hotter and hotter, whipping his back with its scorching rays. But still he kept going. The climb chipped away many minutes. Minutes turned into hours. Finally, when it seemed like his arms were going to break like the frailest of twigs, he looked up once more. He saw that he was almost there.

Matsugoro listened closely to his inner voice. He had to visualize that he had the ability within and remember himself as a child. Just as The Tall One once seemed so indomitable to him, he now felt like the one who was unconquerable.

He allowed a breath. It was such a deep, loving breath and let go of all fear and finally heard the voice.

With his last bit of energy, Matsugoro lifted himself and finally caught sight of the very top branch. He let himself rest awhile. With limbs quivering and sweat dripping, he saw his village. What a sight. Suddenly, everything looked so small. Then the voice of the Monkey Boy traveled from his belly up and he yelled from the top of his lungs: "Thank you." He surrendered to his spirit, returning to the Monkey Boy. The booming, clear voice sounded almost foreign to him, for he hadn't heard it for so long.

He felt aware. A new vision was emerging. His body felt so alive for the first time in years. He was frightened at first, but he realized that he enjoyed this awareness. It really wasn't about this one conquest. There were surely more challenges that awaited Matsugoro. But through this journey, he saw a vista of other possibilities.

The breath that Matsugoro allowed is the key. With that one breath, he lets himself live the moment. The strong Voice is Matsugoro; Matsugoro is the Voice.

Matsugoro's newfound voice reflects who he truly is and not how his culture viewed him.

Matsugoro became empowered through his vision and energized by his step-by-step climb, thus building confidence, self-esteem, and mastery.

Matsugoro makes a choice. The goal is to live life on his terms.

Just as Matsugoro's life journey is defined by The Tall One, so is ours.

Vocal Power

*If you ask me what I came into this world
to do, I will tell you that I came to live out loud.*

—Emile Zola

A couple of years ago, I was hired by the upper
management of an elegant hotel chain to coach
Bob, one of their general managers. The edifice of the
property that this particular gentleman supervised was
grand, sophisticated, and overlooked a breathtaking
vista. An employee had filed a harassment complaint
against Bob for the less than sophisticated behavior of
yelling and cursing to command his staff. Bob was
threatened with the loss of his job. Before I could help
him, however, I knew we would have to identify any
deeper issues that were contributing to his belligerence. He also had to understand and take
responsibility for his role in his predicament.

"Do you want to give your career away?" I asked
him. "If so, then keep on doing what you're doing. If
not, you're ready to begin the Vocal Power journey."
From our initial conversation, I determined that Bob
wasn't a "bad guy." He just had a short fuse. People

around him weren't doing their jobs properly, the hotel was suffering, and he was responsible. Thus, his self-esteem had plummeted to an all-time low. Yet losing his cool and screaming only made things worse. He needed to transform his style of communication, and he had to find a better way to motivate the members of his staff.

Bob and I worked together for about a year. Early on we met a couple of times a month, then once a month, and finally we did only periodic check-ins. Throughout the process we also had intermittent phone lessons. Most importantly, he worked on his own at home and at work everyday, practicing and integrating the exact same vocal techniques that you are going to learn in this book. He practiced releasing his tongue, jaw, and neck tension; breathing more effectively; and slowing down his delivery, becoming conscious while doing so. These and other adjustments affected the pitch of his voice and made him sound warmer, more clearly conveying not just the message but also *the messenger*.

The Vocal Awareness method exercises are the core elements of my program. But the System, as a whole, does much more than improve the sound of your voice. It also improves the "sound" of your inner voice—your thoughts, feelings, and internal guidance. Thus, I also taught Bob how to walk through the hotel and take a few minutes to stop, shake hands, and interact with his employees genuinely, while maintaining eye contact and truly listening to them and to himself.

I told him what I tell all hotel employees with whom I've worked—from the phone operators, the front desk personnel—to the general manager: "Your grand edifice may bring guests in the first time, but it's not what brings them back—genuine, caring service does." In our second meeting, I had Bob spend 45 minutes on video learning how to say—and embody—just one paragraph of the service statement he'd memorized when he began working for the hotel, which basically was to be friendly, welcoming, and attentive to the needs of guests. Initially I heard the words, but I didn't believe what he said because there was no feeling behind them. Soon, however, he paid deeper attention and became conscious of the essence he communicated.

In later meetings, Bob and I set up role-playing sessions where we strategized new and more effective ways he could communicate with different department heads about common problems. He learned the difference between being a perfectionist and striving for excellence. The idea that perfection is possible is a psychological death trap. Excellence, on the other hand, means always doing your best and allowing your best to improve by degrees. He soon found appropriate ways to delegate responsibility to his staff members that prevented him from assuming their burdens. In the process, he defined a persona for himself as a leader and teacher of people. He wanted to be perceived as less brusque and "bossy" and as more of a whole human being, someone who was safe to approach for guidance in conducting the business at hand.

Although Bob was in a tough spot at the hotel, I had no doubt he would turn his career around. Frankly, the tools of Vocal Awareness are incredibly effective. Over the years, they have helped thousands of people learn to hear and see themselves more fully and objectively, and harness that heightened awareness and ability for the purpose of expression. In addition, Bob was diligent, willing, and had set a clear goal. He knew where he was beginning and he knew where he wanted to end up—there had to be a dramatic shift! Through Vocal Awareness, he had the means to get there.

Over the next few months, it was as though Bob became a new person. Of course, one of our goals was to bring out more of who he actually was rather than cover up or change his true identity. Authenticity is a major tenet of Vocal Awareness. His staff soon perceived him as a caring and tolerant authority figure, rather than an abusive authoritarian. As a result, people began to take more responsibility. They worked harder, fewer mistakes were made, money was saved, and business improved.

The president of the company paid the hotel a visit and was dumbfounded at the obvious changes. His response was to give Bob a promotion and an upgrade to a bigger hotel that needed a similar turnaround. Developing Vocal Power earned Bob an industry-wide reputation as a top hotelier. Instead of being forced out of his company, he became a rising star through the embodiment of the Vocal Awareness principles.

What Is Vocal Power?

Right now, you may be wondering why I shared all the details of Bob's story. This book is about the voice, isn't it? The sounds that people make. You may be asking, "What does the voice have to do with eye contact, shaking hands, and self-esteem?" A great deal, I assure you.

Research has shown that in any face-to-face spoken communication, only eight percent of the impact on the listener comes from the words used, 37 percent comes from the tone of voice, and the remaining 55 percent from body language. To have true Vocal Power, you must make a strong impact on your listener on all three of these levels simultaneously. In a telephone conversation, 92 percent of the impact comes from vocal tone and only eight percent from the words that are spoken. Body language is not as significant a factor on the phone, of course, because your listener cannot see you. Nonetheless, it does matter. Sitting slumped over or tensed up affects the sound of your voice. Among other things, it hinders your breathing and lowers your energy.

The statistics above are revealing. But I also find it interesting that in practice, listeners neither experience words, vocal tone, and body language separately nor do speakers experience their acts of communication in this divided manner.

Vocal Power unites the mind/body/spirit. On a mental level, "voice" is the term we use for the act of expression, such as when we "voice" our ideas and opinions. Among other things, it involves the words we choose and the commitment we make to saying them. Because speaking and singing communicate emotions as well as thoughts, unresolved psychological issues can hamper both forms of vocal expression. On a physical level, "voice" is the word we use to describe the sound waves created by the vibration of air through the vocal folds. Making sound is an activity that involves muscles in the throat and abdomen, as well as other parts of the body, and the use of the breath. Unnecessary tension hinders the production of sound.

There is also a spiritual level to voice. It is the intangible energy, or vitality that we project into the world, which originates from the same breath that gives us life. The Latin root of the word spirit is *spiritus*, which means "breath" or "to breathe." *Inspirare* is the verb "to breathe into, to inspire." So, whenever you breathe, you are connecting to your spirit and inspiration.

As you work with the program in *Vocal Power*, every element of your Voice will begin to transform. Not only will you sound better, you'll also look and feel better—less tense and more confident, assured, and, to the best of your ability, in charge of your destiny. You are going to claim ownership of your Self through the integration of your mind/body/spirit. That's why, from now on, I spell "Voice" with a capital "V" when referring to the three levels described above. You may not understand this yet, but my *promise* to you is that your life will change for the better as your Voice—your identity—transforms.

So, how will the Vocal Awareness method improve your mental focus, vocal quality, body language, and self-esteem, among other benefits, all at once? That's a big promise for a program that can be done in as few as seven minutes a day. Let's find out.

The Vocal Awareness Method

Think about the first few times you ever drove a car. Were you nervous or confident, able or inept? Your body hadn't yet absorbed the physical sensations of coordinating several tasks. Therefore, once the car was in motion—and driving in the face of oncoming traffic—you probably made several jerky starts and stops and swerved a bit whenever you tried to do more than one thing at the same time, such as driving while rolling down the window or driving while looking in the rearview mirror.

But I'm sure that ever since your early driving lessons, perhaps circling around a parking lot, you have driven fluidly without having to remind your body how it needs to function. These days, your body seems to "think" before your mind dictates an action. That's because we are thinking-feeling organisms. The Vocal Awareness method recognizes this fact. It is an incredibly effective system because it trains your entire mind/body/spirit—integratively—not *just* the mind, or *just* the body.

There are three reasons why learning to drive is a good analogy for developing Vocal Power. The first parallel, which I just described, has to do with mind/body/spirit integration and how that works. The second is about the process of instruction. And the third has to do with the outcomes we're seeking when we learn how to do anything, as well as the essence of ability and accomplishment. Let's consider the second way now.

How did you learn to drive? Were you self-reliant or did you need an instructor? (That's a leading question, since nobody learns to drive without help.) Even though you may have read a manual explaining the features of your vehicle, someone had to teach you to adjust the seat and mirror; where the gas and brake pedals were and what they did; how to turn on the ignition; hold the steering wheel; turn on the wipers, blinkers, radio, air conditioner, and defroster. Someone had to teach you to look in the mirror, turn your head before pulling away from the curb, put your hands in the "ten and two" positions on the steering wheel, and do everything else you now take for granted. For a while, I bet your instructor sat next to you whenever you drove, reminding you of the right procedures to follow and in what order. You literally didn't have to think for yourself.

Soon, you became an able driver. You no longer needed an instructor to remind you what to do. You passed your driver's test, got a license, and became a daily commuter or a weekend traveler. These days you can therefore cruise the highway safely—almost on "remote control"—because a physical intelligence has taken over management of the whole driving operation. Driving has become habitual. As long as you get from point A to point B, you're fine.

Which gets me to my third point. If you are like

most people, the way you habitually drive is comparable to the habitual way you communicate.
Ordinarily, you don't stop and remind yourself to
breathe a certain way or to stand or sit in a specific
posture when you're speaking. You also probably don't
pay much attention to the quality of sound you're
producing or even necessarily to the words you've
chosen to get your point across. In essence, you lack
awareness.

But that's about to change as you apply the Vocal
Awareness method.

Actually, most people lack awareness in everything
they do—not just in driving or communicating. Lots
of folks have never learned how to instruct themselves
as carefully as their driving instructors once did. They
never learned self-reliance. The Vocal Awareness
method teaches self-reliance, awareness, and many
other important qualities.

Okay, for some reason—and everybody's is
different—you now believe your Voice is holding you
back. Or you simply want to be the best you can be.
Frankly, you haven't picked up this book in order to
learn how to speak in an ordinary way. You're interested in this program because you want a better than
average Voice. Being an adequate communicator is no
longer enough for you. You want your Voice to reflect
your greater aspirations and your innermost Self.

What would you do if you decided you wanted to drive like a racecar driver? An expert driver! You would enroll in a special school that teaches Formula One drivers. You would aim to break your old driving habits and form new and more effective ones. You'd go back to the basics and start paying attention to every tiny detail of your performance. You would establish a discipline of doing laps around a racecourse until your heightened abilities were second nature.

In a while, the same integration would occur that enabled you to first drive a car fluidly; however, this time you would not let what you were doing become subconscious. You would keep evaluating your results and making adjustments in a continuous effort to improve the outcome, then apply those new skills when you were out on the highway. You wouldn't be satisfied unless you were a more confident and capable driver.

Can you see that one part of becoming an expert is purely technical and pertains to building your biome-chanical skills and concentration? But that another important part is your decision and commitment to rise to the level of your expectations? The latter involves showing up to do what is necessary. This may seem obvious when you're looking at a sport or the arts but is less apparent in terms of your own Voice. Nonetheless, they are equally fundamental parts of developing Vocal Power.

Interestingly, every successful athlete I've ever taught has told me that 90 percent of the game they play is mental—that's their winning edge. Former Buffalo Bills wide receiver Andre Reed, the third best pass receiver of all-time, commented to me on the importance of this advantage in football. He said, "Some athletes may be younger or bigger, but nobody is mentally tougher than I am." This quality helped make him great.

The Vocal Awareness method is a training program for more effective communication. Like learning to drive well, it is a discipline that coordinates mental focus and technical skills until they become so ingrained in the physical body that you can deliberately and consciously call upon them at any time, even—if not especially—when you're under pressure. In the process, you impel yourself to overcome fear and doubt—even when these are nonspecific. And no matter what your vocal and communication habits are when you begin, your best Voice will always be evolving and getting even better so long as you continue practicing the Vocal Awareness techniques. Furthermore, you act as your own instructor in the process. Learning how to be a supportive and compassionate coach is tremendously important—it's even life altering!

Are you familiar with the concept of a paradigm

shift? A paradigm is a model or belief that is considered absolute and underscores everything in a system. When it changes, everything else in that system changes. For instance, the belief that the world was flat was a paradigm for centuries; when it shifted to "the world is round," the new paradigm affected transportation, trade, culture, and humanity's relationship to the cosmos. Space flight would not be possible if we still believed the world was flat.

Well, *the Vocal Awareness method is a paradigm shift*. It's similar to getting your computer upgraded. New software makes every application and the whole system run more effectively. Another realm of possibilities and breakthroughs is opened up. By practicing the vocal workout described in Chapter 4, not only will your Voice improve, but you'll also find parallel changes occurring in other areas of your life that you might not have originally anticipated. These include developing a more positive outlook, feeling more physical vitality, and having more confidence in confrontational situations.

The vocal workout will help you accomplish a complete personal transformation. Through a series of sound-making and biomechanical warm-up exercises, you will deepen and free your breathing; engender relaxation in your tongue, jaw, neck, and shoulders; and strengthen your larynx (a.k.a. the voice box), so that the sound of your voice improves. Simultaneously, you'll learn how to sharpen your concentration, move through and beyond your emotional obstacles, and connect to your higher purpose in life. Through the mind/body/spirit trinity of Vocal Awareness, you'll learn how to apply these same techniques continuously to any text, song, or other "performance" material you're planning to use, even words you're going to say to your boss or spouse, or during everyday encounters. Thus, your Voice—you—will be powerfully enhanced on every level.

What Are the Benefits?

There are immense benefits to participating in the Vocal Awareness method. Because it integrates mind/body/spirit, you'll find that these techniques have the potential to:

♪ Alleviate common vocal and communication problems, such as the fear of public speaking, using a high "little girl" voice or a weak ineffectual male voice, and vocal tension, among other issues;

♪ Improve your physical health, for instance, by relieving severe jaw tension (also known as "TMJ"), hoarseness, and tension, among other conditions;

♪ Raise your endorphin levels;

♪ Enhance your body language and correct poor posture, while easing back problems and other tension-related conditions;

♪ Enable you to claim ownership of your Self;

♪ Liberate your singing voice.

I have devoted a separate chapter in *Vocal Power* to each one of these vital topics and will use many true stories to illustrate their connections to the vocal workout.

How Long Does it Take to Learn?

The beauty of the Vocal Awareness method is that it is incredibly simple. There is no reason why it should be complicated. Even though it is a detailed program and trains you to notice subtle distinctions, you can actually learn to do the Vocal Awareness techniques in a few hours and will begin to experience the benefit immediately. In fact, if you start today and spend only seven minutes doing the vocal exercises every morning for the next seven days, by the end of the week there will be a notable improvement in the quality of your Voice and your ability to have an impact on your listeners and your Self. So although these exercises are easy to learn, remember, and practice, they are also extremely effective and will produce profound and lasting results.

If there is anything that makes this program seem complicated, it is what goes on between our ears. On occasion, our habits and history as human beings make learning, unveiling, and revealing seem daunting. Many times, we would prefer to maintain established patterns of behavior that give us the illusion of security. However, as you shall realize in future chapters and by following the program, the program's design is a wonderful—and even enjoyable—framework for confronting our personal inhibitions.

Over the years, I have worked with many significant performers, broadcasters, and athletes, as well as corporations and "regular civilians." I have found that although even the most highly successful people do not necessarily feel emotionally secure, they have all made the choice to empower themselves. It's a commitment that must continuously be renewed, a contract that must always be renegotiated. With every step, they weigh their alternatives and essentially ask the same question: Does this empower me, or does this disempower me? Acting out of their empowerment separates the best from the rest. Remember: Any time you make a *conscious* choice to move toward your goals it is only how badly you want it and what you're requiring your Self to do that really matters—not how scary, intimidating, or seemingly daunting your choice may be.

We are not our behaviors.

Let's get started. In Bob's story at the beginning of the chapter, I wrote, "He knew where he was beginning and he knew where he wanted to end up." You're going to begin your own Vocal Power journey with the same activity he did: *choosing a persona.*

ACTIVITY:
Choosing Your Persona

Do you recall that in the Introduction I told you the secret of Vocal Power is taking charge of how you are perceived—not just by others but also by yourself? In English, the word "persona" refers to someone's character or how others view that individual. Psychologically, it has the connotation of a protective façade. But this concept actually originated from ancient Greek dramas where the actors wore masks with pursed lips that helped them project sound to their audiences. The root is the ancient Etruscan word "phersu," which literally means "through the sound."

Thus, it has long been recognized that identity is conveyed vocally. Instead of being a way to disguise your Self and hide, your persona is the truth of your identity being revealed and projected outward. As you learn the Vocal Awareness method, you literally are going to learn how to select and change your persona or the image you portray to your Self and to the world. Ultimately, you will become that person.

In my workshops, I often ask a student who plays tennis for recreation to come forward. I have the student serve once, and he usually just goes through the basic motions. Then I set up a scenario, such as "You're playing in a tournament for charity and somehow got to a second set tiebreaker against Andre Agassi. Suddenly you're aware that no one in the stands wants you to win because he's the champion." I have my student feel the anxiety and pressure, saying, "The tennis racquet feels like a lead weight and the tennis ball looks like the size of a pea," and then I ask him to show me the movements of his serve. This serve is usually inhibited and the student holds his breath.

But then I'll have him serve a third time using the same scenario, only with different instructions. "Don't come back to the baseline until you truly see yourself as a champion serving an ace." The improvement is always notable. The student's body does everything with more attention, focus, and care—and he also breathes. You see that the same student with the same exact skills can radically enhance his technical proficiency simply by choosing the identity he wants to embody. The lesson here is that our perceptions shape reality. The way we think or feel about anything we do literally changes the way it is. I change the scenario; the student changes his behavior.

Now, the first step before you can make any changes in your Voice is to ask two questions. Please write down your answers. You can always update and refine them.

♪ How do I believe I am presently perceived?

♪ How would I like to be perceived?

This is important, so be honest about present perceptions. Then, get very clear about the level of excellence you are striving to attain and the qualities you want to embody. Keep in mind that this is your *all-the-time* identity, not just your identity at work or in your social life. This is how you want to be perceived by everybody rather than by a few people in only a few places.

Write your new persona statement in one or two complete sentences—not a list of bullet points. Include positive concepts only. It may read, "I want to be perceived as secure, successful, and confident—a strong leader." The punctuation at the end will either be a period or an exclamation point. "I want to be perceived as warm and approachable, and an inspiring and courageous teacher of human potential!" "I want to be perceived as a visionary investment manager." In addition, do not write in any parenthetical caveats that detract from the force of your persona statement, such as "I want to be perceived as a [fill in the blank]—except when I'm nervous or don't feel like it." Your new persona should be an all-the-time identity.

Now, spend a bit of time drawing two pictures, one representing your current persona and the other representing your new persona. These may be abstract or lifelike, simple or complex. This task helps you communicate with your subconscious mind to bring up feelings and conceptions that may lie beneath the surface of your awareness. Don't worry about your talents as an artist; no one will ever see your drawings but you.

Can You Really Reach Empowerment Through Your Voice?

When I was a young man, you couldn't have found my self-esteem with a large observatory telescope, simply because it didn't exist. For a while I didn't have the courage to show up as Arthur. I was like a groundhog. I'd see my own shadow and dart back into my hole for another six weeks of winter. Nonetheless, I had the integrity to practice my singing and showed up as my Self more and more until I was ultimately comfortable being me. The discoveries I made led me to create the Vocal Awareness method you are now beginning. Having gone through the Vocal Power journey, I can assure you that although you may feel odd initially, like you're doing an impression of Pinocchio dancing on his strings, soon you'll *feel* and actually *be* more authentic and natural.

At first, living up to your new persona statement may seem a bit intimidating. Perhaps you'll think, "Who am I kidding? I feel phony. No one's going to believe this." Just remember: This is the beginning of a process to help you embody what you say you want to convey. Give it a chance. Surrender to the process. Many people have a misunderstanding about the nature of surrender, believing it indicates weakness or being on the losing side in a battle. In fact, the word is derived from Middle French and means "to yield" or "to give back." Surrender is actually about being flexible and generous. For this Work, surrender is both a spiritual and psychological necessity.

I have taught four Olympic gold medalists—from track and field, speed skating, and gymnastics—who were becoming broadcasters and public speakers. To achieve athletic success, they had all practiced eight hours a day, 365 days of the year. I always made a point to ask, "Do you know that you are extraordinary?" And their typical reply was, "No, I've become a machine. I was supposed to win." They didn't yet know who they were when they weren't wearing red, white, and blue and bringing home medals for America. Their persona statements enabled them to begin to discover their value outside their roles and activities. I call this an *identity without labels*.

These athletes found Vocal Power by establishing their persona statements and applying the Vocal Awareness techniques that supported them. Then they were able to reveal their identities as more complete people: funny, smart, warm, and courageous—their full Selves, not just their machine-like selves.

Matt Fong, a former California State Treasurer who, in his capacity as a reservist, currently consults with Senior Air Force Leadership at the Pentagon, is another student of mine. He contacted me in 1999, shortly after he ran a close race for the United States Senate, only losing narrowly to Senator Barbara Boxer. In our first conversation, he told me he realized that he'd lost the election in part because he was not as effective of a communicator as he could be. But he didn't want to lose future opportunities to lead and make a contribution to society.

Since that time, Matt has developed true Vocal Power. I hardly know anyone as passionately dedicated to his work as Matt. He had an epiphany while drafting his persona statement. For the first time in his life, he was able to focus on *who* he is rather than *what* he does. It was as though he had pointed a compass and moved due north. Even though his Vocal Power journey continues—which they always do—he chooses not to view what he still needs to learn as daunting or unattainable. He is always willing to address issues that come up in the process of replacing his old vocal and presentational habits. The reward for this effort comes from communicating his messages well, thus making an even more significant contribution.

I have also worked with many celebrated performers—most commonly actors and singers—whose dedication to their crafts is inspiring. Developing Vocal Power has been an asset to their careers because it contributed to their artistry. I'd like to share a couple of these stories with you here.

At the beginning of her career at age 18, I worked with Academy Award-winning actress Angelina Jolie. She had known since childhood that she wanted to be an actress. She already possessed the fearlessness and fierce individuality that are her hallmarks, and she had the willingness to connect to her emotions. Practicing the Vocal Awareness exercises strengthened her vocal muscles so that she could create effortless, uninhibited, sensual sound. She wrote a persona statement. We set out to create a Voice that reflected it, one that held unlimited vocal nuances for the myriad of characters she would portray. As she developed Vocal Power, she learned to tap into more of her vocal energy and expanded her range of expression. Although there have assuredly been many other steps in her journey of empowerment, I know Angelina's Vocal Power contributed to her later success.

Actor Pierce Brosnan and I first worked together on developing his Voice when he was making the television series *Remington Steele* early in his career, and I have coached him off and on since then. In 1998, he called upon my services when he played the title role in *Grey Owl*, a biographical film directed by Sir Richard Attenborough. To portray the character of Archibald Belaney effectively, he knew he needed to sublimate his own identity and adopt a new persona extremely different from his own. Interestingly, that's also basically what Belaney had done. He was an Englishman who grew up fascinated with Native American culture. He moved to Canada in the mid-1900s, reinvented himself as an Ojibway Indian, and lived as a trapper and guide. He dyed his hair and skin brown and took the surname Grey Owl. Even though he became a prominent environmentalist who traveled to meet King George VI in order to preserve the Canadian beavers, the public never penetrated his disguise until after his death.

Pierce earnestly wanted to *be* Grey Owl. This meant courageously surrendering to the Vocal Awareness process and allowing the Work to take place even when he didn't understand it or it made him feel uncomfortable. We would discuss, "What would a man who lived in the wilderness sound like and walk like?" and then embody the answers. For instance, there would be no tension around the lips. In truly going after the character—the persona—there could be no barriers. As a result of Pierce's commitment and surrender to the *Work*, an interesting development took place. Pierce gained human benefits by learning Archie's technical skills, such as canoeing and shooting a bow and arrow. Every skill he learned enhanced his own life as he integrated it within his mind/body/spirit. This illustrates my earlier point: *We truly cannot "act" a persona without becoming it.*

When I was the vocal director on the movie *Annie,* a musical based on the classic comic strip and directed by John Huston, I worked with the talented young star Aileen Quinn, selected for the role after the producers auditioned 8,200 girls. She was nine years old, weighed about 45 pounds, and had an octave and a half singing range. We initially met on a Monday and she could barely hit the highest note in the title song "Tomorrow." When she sang, her head quivered with tension. That Thursday, Aileen had her first recording session. She then had a head cold. However, by using the Vocal Awareness techniques, she had increased her range to three and a half octaves and had no tension or head shaking. With my assistance in the recording booth, she sang "Tomorrow" in one take.

Later in the book, I will go into more details about this project, as it was a breakthrough in my professional teaching career. Through it I met and worked with Albert Finney, Sean Connery, Carol Burnett, and other celebrated performers. It led to many more opportunities. For now, suffice it to say that the producer of the film, Joe Layton, a director and choreographer who had won two Tony Awards for his productions on Broadway, was so impressed with Aileen's accomplishment that he came up to me a few days later and said, "You are masterful! May I study with you?" Both he and Aileen continued studying with me for many years, and a true friendship developed as well.

Taking the Next Step

The journey we take in Vocal Awareness is never outward toward accomplishments but always and only inward toward discovery of the deeper Self. When we explore Voice, we tap into our own power. The goal is personal sovereignty, meaning "supreme excellence or an example of it." My promise in this book is that you'll learn how to achieve sovereignty. You will be led consistently to expand the parameters of your identity and to fulfill your most heartfelt dreams and desires. If the eyes are the windows to the soul, then the Voice is the window of the soul that has opened up.

When we speak, information is always being conveyed by the body's "broadcast" systems. To be conscious and in charge or unconscious of the signals that are being sent and received is our choice. While speaking, we open up and reveal ourselves, communicating our innermost Selves to the outer world. At the same time, we offer our thoughts, whether simple or profound, personal or general, to the threat of judgment. We thereby risk parental, social, and public censure—or acceptance. Yes, that, too, can seem risky! There is always the possibility that our ideas may not be accepted. There is always the threat that *we* may not be accepted. And if our ideas and we *are* accepted—what happens then? In the next chapter, I will address how common vocal and communication challenges stem from these issues.

2 Common Vocal and Communication Challenges

Fear can only be driven out by a strong awareness of the value of life.
—Dorothy L. Sayers

Recently, I began working with a gentleman who is supposed to make public appearances as an aspect of his job. Yet he is deathly afraid of public speaking and always defers this task to someone else, even when he knows the appearance would only last two to five minutes. All that is usually required on such occasions is to offer a simple "thank you" as he accepts an award on behalf of his boss and organization. But the mere thought of sitting near the podium waiting to be introduced makes him feel as though the air is being sucked out of him. For the same reason, he also avoids speaking up in meetings of more than a few people. Whenever he is about to contribute to the discussion, it's as though he's falling into a deep abyss of self-doubt. He worries that he'll stammer and make embarrassing mistakes. Until lately, he simply avoided dealing with the problem. Then he finally got fed up and came to see me.

In an early session, before he even opened his mouth to work on the one paragraph sample speech I had asked him to prepare, I had him imagine what it would be like to wait to be introduced at a typical event. But I gave him some proactive substitutions for his usual worrying. He practiced saying Thank You to His Source, sitting in stature, and allowing a Silent, Loving, Down-through-his-body Breath. (You'll learn these same Vocal Awareness techniques, as well as others, in the next chapter.) I also had him visualize the room he would be in. When he stood up to walk to the pretend lectern that I'd set up in my studio, I asked him to remain aware of his posture. Then before delivering his speech, he consciously stood in silence for just a moment and *allowed* another deep breath. Having these defined, compassionate activities on which to focus reduced his anxiety substantially. But there was more to it than this; Vocal Awareness is also about paying attention to detail.

The first time he said his speech aloud in my studio, his energy was low and he made mistakes. He said his name but didn't mention his title or organization. In fact, he'd even neglected to include them in his speech. He tried to paraphrase the text he'd written instead of reading it verbatim. His head dipped down and he avoided looking out toward me, his audience. During our session that day, I had him repeat the speech several more times. My notes indicated he was to do it word for word, be louder and louder, look up from the page to connect, and take his time. Because the sound of his voice felt "big" and "mechanical" to him, he had practically been whispering. Together we identified and underlined the most emotional words in the text, so he could emphasize these when speaking. My student agreed to practice the Vocal Awareness techniques at home everyday and also use them on his job as much as possible.

A few weeks later, during his lesson, he excitedly informed me of a spontaneous breakthrough experience. He'd been sitting in a meeting and had something so important to contribute that it drove him to speak up. Even though he felt uncomfortable, he took his time and used the tools of Vocal Awareness that we'd explored together in my studio. He got his idea across without stammering or humiliating himself, and he felt that he was actually heard and respected. A colleague came up to him afterwards and confirmed, "What you said today was vital." He would never have been willing to take the risk of being "sucked out into the void" if he hadn't been consciously taking the journey to realize Vocal Power.

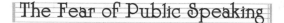

The Fear of Public Speaking

Sociologists will tell you that the greatest fear in our society is the fear of public speaking. They say that it ranks higher than the fear of death, accidents, and criminal acts. It poses a major threat, doesn't it? It is not trivial. It can even trigger physical responses, such as heart palpitations, profuse sweating, and nausea. The size and importance of the audience seem to magnify normally low-grade anxieties. Why?

The fear of public speaking is a misnomer. In actuality, people suffer from two distinct fears that have been lumped together: *the fear of abandonment* and *the fear of owning our power*. More properly, the second could be called "the fear of what you might think of me *while* I am owning my power or being my Self." (How would we ever know anyway? After all, we can't read people's minds.) Many of us would prefer to remain invisible and unheard since we believe that if we reveal ourselves, there might be unpleasant consequences, such as humiliation, ridicule, and rejection. We fear that we're not enough—and would rather keep it a secret.

Some of us are afraid of claiming our personal power in public since we believe that greater responsibility might fall upon us than we are prepared to handle or that doing well could provoke an attack or envy. If we claimed our full talents and abilities, life would also change. Then we'd have to move out of our "comfort zone" and into the unknown.

Two of my students are perfect examples of what I'm talking about. The first is a businessman whom I've been coaching for a while. He is supremely gifted in many ways. Recently he's been looking more deeply at himself, such as undergoing an intimate exploration through journaling, and learning how to claim his gifts more fully. He is striving to grow and be a good human being, and to lead a life of balance. By exploring the concept of humility, he has discovered that he's been falsely humble. It seemed blasphemous to him to claim his abilities. "Why me?" he would ask. "Why do I have a talent that other people don't? Doesn't everyone have this ability? Are you sure?" I helped him see that by denying his gifts he was disenabling himself and also keeping Vocal Power at arm's length.

To acknowledge your truth is not arrogant; to not acknowledge it is.

I also have a singing student who happens to be a voice teacher herself. She has a wonderful vocal instrument. For the past two years, I've been acting as her midwife as she strives to record her first album of original songs. Even though she has a wonderful talent, she frequently holds it back from the world, in part because of her fear of what other people might think when she claims it. She also has issues with her voice not being "perfect" enough, when in fact she sings with wonderful humanity and has a terrific voice. But remember—perception is reality. This is an exercise in frustration. I joke to her: "We're at seven centimeters in the birth canal. But you may come out breech now, because you're making it so difficult."

Can you see that the ideas above are excuses we use to abdicate responsibility for our lives? We often sublimate our power to the power of our projections. Projections are ideas about our Selves, the world, the people to whom we're talking, how things are "supposed" to be, and so forth. They are not absolute. They are an interpretation of the past and future.

Here's another example from my own life. When I was in my early 30s, I was afraid of becoming "too famous" as a voice teacher. If I got too much work and needed to travel, maybe I would be separated from my wife and two young sons. This projection held me back from wholeheartedly pursuing jobs that involved travel until I realized I could take my family with me. Then I never looked back!

ACTIVITY:
Your Naked Voice

Before you go any further, please do an unusual exercise. I want you to go home (if you're not already there) where you can have complete privacy, take out your tape recorder, and then make two recordings of your voice. For the first recording, recite a poem and then sing a song—both of your own choosing. When you make the second recording, I want you to repeat the same poem and sing the same song, but this time without wearing any clothes. Then listen to the tape and compare the two versions. What do you hear? Big differences? Subtle differences? Which versions of the poem and song do you prefer?

I often give my students this activity as a homework assignment early in our work together. When they bring the tape to me for listening, I am always able to identify two different voices. Sometimes the singing voice is more on pitch, or it is sweeter. Sometimes the speaking voice is more communicative, warmer, slower, or richer. But one voice is always better—and that voice is the unclothed or *naked voice*.

The naked voice represents the inner child or the authentic Self that we think needs to be protected. The *clothed voice* represents the part of Self that is parenting or protecting us. This parental aspect is concerned with the outer world and its social strictures, whereas the childlike aspect retains the essence of honesty and love for life that we all have in childhood. The parent is afraid to let other people see who we really are—the child. But the naked voice betrays the unique and special selfhood that is ours, which does not need to cover up or guard itself with defensiveness or live with fear.

The lesson here is that we don't need to cover and protect in the way that we're used to; we can allow ourselves to be more liberated than we thought possible.

Are You Hiding Behind Your Habits?

In the workplace, we might feel our breath caught in our throat when we go into a meeting or feel we have to swallow our pride and say, "Yes, sir," and "No, ma'am," even though we don't agree or feel that we're being forced to put up with compromising situations. At home, we might grind our teeth instead of telling our spouses what's really on our minds or sharing our feelings. The perception is that there is no choice, and we have to settle for the way it is. Revealing our true thoughts, feelings, and needs—using our Voices— seems too risky.

Most vocal and communication challenges stem

from different kinds of anxiety. Our society is hierarchical and largely patriarchal. There is so much abuse of power and privilege—men abuse women, parents abuse children, straights abuse gays, race abuses race, people with status brandish their wills over those beneath them—that we often do not feel safe or valued for being who we are. Therefore, many of us would prefer to hide. In an effort to cope, we develop protective habits and inhibitions. Protective behaviors often emerge of their own accord, and most of the time we don't even know that we're doing them.

It takes a lot of courage to live life and to reveal our innermost feelings and convictions—first to our Selves and then to others, and I have great admiration for those who develop the capacity to take risks. Yet I would never judge anyone for taking however much time they need to be prepared for a risk. Today, there is scientific research that demonstrates how strong or conflicted emotions can manifest themselves in the body. Almost everybody has had an occasional sleepless night when they were worried or upset and knows the gut sensation of queasiness or indigestion when events go terribly wrong. Back pain has been linked to anger, and hives have been linked to stress. We must not ignore the direct messages the body sends us. As you enter into the Vocal Awareness method, you will learn to honor and respect your feelings and insights as you gain the practical tools you need to move safely through your current limits.

Let me reiterate the point that none of these behaviors are thought through. If your inner voice tends to be critical, please realize that it can be scary for everyone to make a dream become a reality. Otherwise, so many people wouldn't share this dilemma. We are not "cowards" or "losers" when we avoid those experiences we fear; we are simply being human. And frankly, those harsh assessments or judgments are a big part of the problem. In addition to the ways I already mentioned, people's fears result in other symptoms that affect their ability to communicate. See how many apply to you:

♪ Physical tension (especially in the tongue, jaw, neck, and shoulders);

♪ Cracking voices;

♪ Freezing up;

♪ Trembling;

♪ Mouth dryness;

♪ Dizziness;

♪ High, "little girl" female voices;

♪ Weak, ineffectual male voices;

♪ Belligerence and loudness;

♪ Profuse swearing;

♪ Harsh internal judgments;

♪ Feelings of inferiority and "not good enough";

♪ Mumbling.

Although you may be relying right now on vocal habits, such as breathiness and a clenched jaw, and certain patterns of behavior, such as averting your eyes to protect yourself unconsciously, it is only because you don't yet know another, more effective way. Understand this is not a judgment, merely an observation. The habits and inhibitions you've developed, you thought, originally served a real purpose, which was to keep you safe somehow or to be acceptable—everyone's reason is different—however, they now limit you. But that's about to change.

In Vocal Awareness, we learn to accept where we are but never settle for it.

The Vocal Awareness method will give you the opportunity to replace the old ineffective habits with more effective ones. As you'll soon discover, that's the reason why it includes elements, such as nurturing thoughts and loving breaths. It will help you live life on your own terms, feel safe in every encounter, be confident, enjoy being who you are, and not apologize

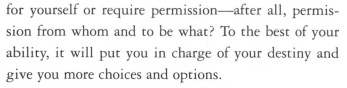

for yourself or require permission—after all, permission from whom and to be what? To the best of your ability, it will put you in charge of your destiny and give you more choices and options.

It is important to acknowledge that in some instances, vocal and communication problems do pertain to certain motor challenges, such as lisping, stuttering, and more severe disorders. These issues will be addressed in greater detail in Chapter 5. Suffice it to say for now that people often experience anxiety and low self-esteem when these occur. The Vocal Awareness method is a reliable method for working on a motor challenge and its ancillary emotional aspects.

Our habitual behaviors do not have to be who we are. We act in ways that make us feel safe and comfortable. Perhaps for the first time in your life, you are being asked and given the opportunity to *choose the most effective, most authentic behavior possible*. From now on, please strive for masterful choices.

The Fear of Abandonment

When we experience a sense of abandonment as adults, we are usually tapping into feelings that come from a childhood event. Maybe a teacher intimidated us in class, or we got bullied on the playground. When

I was in sixth grade, I auditioned for the school choir because I loved music. I was asked to sing "America the Beautiful," but because I couldn't sing on pitch, I was rejected and told I was *"tone deaf."* It was devastating, but I am grateful that I didn't let it crush my desire to sing. A year later, I auditioned for a different singing group, Mrs. Grill's Hi-Tones, and was accepted. Besides my family, singing and Voice have been the major focus of my life ever since. Everything I do is informed through my art. I see myself as an artist, teacher, and businessman.

One of my students experienced a similar childhood event but with a less happy outcome—until after we met. She came to see me because she'd been cast in a production of a musical and hadn't sung a note in 20 years. I stood her near the piano and stuck the sheet music for "The Rose" by Amanda McBroom in front of her. While looking in a mirror, she worked on the song for half an hour using the Vocal Awareness techniques. As she was decompressing afterward, she started to sob. I had been able to help her release some jaw tension, experience several musical and vocal successes, and clearly observe her reflection. She then explained that when she was a little girl she had sung at a family event with two of her cousins. Afterward her mother had told her: "You look funny when you sing." Sadly, this thoughtless comment had impacted her throughout her entire life. But she was liberated from it—just like that!

Yes, there were still vestigial remains—or shadows—of her former feelings. She was emotionally and intellectually liberated, but now had to reprogram herself—consciously and conscientiously—to learn new ways of behaving and also what to do with her subsequent freedom.

It is important to understand that even though we fear rejection and abandonment from others, we are the ones actually doing the abandoning and rejecting through the vocal habits we have developed for protection. We often disempower our Selves through the ways we speak.

There are all sorts of ways we might do this. Some examples are:

♪ Speaking very rapidly because you're afraid you can't hold a listener's attention until the end of your sentence (i.e., not taking your time);

♪ Running out of air while talking because you don't breathe deep enough;

♪ Beginning a sentence with energy and then trailing off;

♪ Interjecting a lot of nonwords, such as "um" and "er," or nonmeaningful phrases, such as "you know" and "like" into your statements;

♪ Frequently looking away when you are speaking or listening to someone else;

♪ Giggling a lot, even when you are having a serious conversation;

♪ Panicking in confrontational situations, and in response tightening your neck, shoulders, tongue, and jaw;

♪ Slouching on your chair, or standing hunched over;

♪ Fidgeting and frequently shifting around.

When we speak and carry ourselves in ways that disempower us, it is because we are avoiding a potential consequence, supposed outcome, or feeling that we have projected into the situation. Remember: Our listeners do not *make* us act in these ways. These habits come from within us. We choose them.

Interestingly, we often create what we fear. Take the case of a former student of mine, a young man who was very shy. He was interested in dating a girl who lived down the hall from him, but every time he saw her he got flustered and backed away. By not taking the risk of approaching her, he was never threatened with her possible rejection and the possible hurt it might cause him. Because of his projection that she would reject him, he rejected himself. He created the outcome. I helped him understand that we can create a new relationship to anything we fear by choosing to see it as an opportunity for growth.

Together, we worked on Vocal Power and especially the ways he could allow conscious *Silent, Loving, Down-through-his-body Breaths* and simply *let go* in those moments when he was judging himself poorly. Gradually, he began to surrender to the moment, and ultimately he felt ready to take the risk of revealing his feelings directly to the girl he liked. I recommended that he go and knock on her door. To get past the inhibitions that his mind had created, he could simply count to three and just take the leap.

When he reported back to me, he told me that he had stood outside her door for a full hour before he finally got up his courage. Then he applied the breathing and letting go tools he learned from the Vocal Awareness exercises, counted to three, and knocked. Much to his surprise, she was receptive to his invitation. They went out on a date and subsequently developed a meaningful relationship.

I had a similar experience of working through the projections of my own mind when, about 20 years ago, I attended a screening of a film directed by the actress

Marsha Mason. A student of mine, who had starred in the film, introduced me to her, which was a great opportunity that I almost missed. For after a quick handshake and congratulations, I walked away. Then I surreptitiously circled back and offered a few more banal comments. But I didn't want to be perceived as invasive, so I nearly left it at that. As I walked away the second time, I thought, *You chicken! Don't you realize it's okay to speak to this woman?* I went back over a third time and said, "I have something that I believe will have value for you. I want to teach you Vocal Awareness. May I call you about it?" She said, "Yes," and gave me her phone number. Soon after speaking on the phone, she became my student.

Everything in life revolves around only two things: to choose to do something or to choose not to do it.

Now you have a choice. You can choose to go down your path, like a racehorse, doing what you're told or expected to do with blinders on, unaware, not using your peripheral vision, tuning out, and shutting down. Or you can develop Vocal Power. You can learn to speak to those whose behavior offends you, explain how it makes you feel, and recognize that the behaviors are theirs and do not emanate from you. You can leave situations that harm you. You can also rise above uncomfortable circumstances and perhaps inspire those around you. Once you begin to practice the Vocal Awareness method, there will no longer be a valid reason to shut down, hide, or disempower your Self in any situation.

Yes, you could argue that sometimes people have to make less than ideal choices. For instance, just to get up and suddenly quit your job when you have mouths to feed at home could be a mistake, so you must stay in your job. However, if you choose to stay while planning an exit strategy, you have empowered your Self. The difference is that you are creating your own security and valuing your Self. The Vocal Power techniques will help you to be empowered without stripping you bare or making you feel defenseless. They provide a compassionate and supportive framework.

The Fear of Ownership

When we were children, we played make-believe. However, it wasn't make-believe for us; it was real. We *were* kings and queens holding court and heroes and heroines fighting dragons on our adventures. We *were* bold and invincible. Even though these stories took place in the realm of the imagination, they felt true to life. That was our reality. Then somewhere along the line we gave up the ability to assume any role we chose. We settled for ordinary reality instead of taking the hero's journey. The good news is that we can form a connection with that inner ability to imagine and then *become* someone magnificent and strong. All the small rituals—the daily choices we make—enable the big ones to come true. We don't have to learn a new skill; we only have to reclaim the one we let slip away.

In my work, I have created a character that I call the "Pragmatic Visionary." I've always pictured this person—a man or a woman—in dramatic imagery, as a great knight riding a huge white steed, sword and shield at the ready, prepared to do battle with the metaphorical demons we all confront on a daily basis. Like the knight's path, our paths through life are fraught with challenges, and we need our courageous, empowered personas, who are visionary and can get things done, to help us on our ways. The Pragmatic Visionary teaches us how to take the journey to Vocal Power and how to ensure its success.

You might ask: What is the difference between a dreamer and a pragmatic visionary? A dreamer only dreams a dream. But a pragmatic visionary also works to make the dream come true. That's where the Vocal Awareness method can help.

Not long ago, I worked with a middle-aged man

who had worked his way through the corporate ranks and was being considered for a position as chief financial officer ("CFO") of a large company. He wanted to develop Vocal Power in order to bolster his success and especially to address the regional accent he had acquired while growing up. He knew he was mispronouncing words in a manner that reflected neither his intelligence nor his education, but he was rarely aware of it until after he had already uttered them. Then it made him feel awkward and inferior—less than the best of himself. Because he often felt reticent to speak, he wasn't as effective a leader as he could have been.

Frankly, this is an extremely common vocal problem. But having an accent or difficulty in correctly articulating words is not the real crux of the matter. The real challenge is the inability to hear your own Voice and make a conscious choice about how it comes out. Remember: Our parents and schools do not teach us how to notice and observe ourselves as we are taught when we're learning a sport or performance art. In weight training and in dance, you look at your reflection in the mirror and learn to notice your alignment. In "real" life, we often are specifically taught *not* to notice! In fact, when we pay too much attention to ourselves we may be chastised, "Don't boast!" "That's arrogant!" "Who are you kidding?" "Get over yourself!"

A secondary but no less important issue is how having an accent or mispronouncing words makes you feel when you're speaking and what subconscious habits you have picked up so that you don't have to confront those unpleasant feelings head on. The Vocal Awareness method is not simply speech therapy or vocal rehabilitation to train you to be a perfect enunciator. It does teach that, when necessary, but that's not the ultimate goal. This program works because it will help you listen more closely—and without barraging your Self with the kind of harsh judgments that caused my student to prefer to remain silent.

One day in a phone session, that same student told me that during a meeting, he had finally clearly heard himself mispronouncing certain words we had discussed. He was excited by his discovery although it also brought up some sadness. I reminded him to act lovingly toward himself and use his daily vocal workouts to show himself compassion and respect. You'll learn the same seven empowerment rituals in the next chapter that he used to reduce the internal pressure he was putting on himself. He got the job he was seeking and continued working on Vocal Power. Since then, he has been slowly revealing his Voice more frequently at the office. This has made him a more capable communicator, and he also feels more assured in his role as CFO.

Let's return for a moment to the issue of public speaking. No matter what the psychological issues are behind your own fear of public speaking or how it affects you physically, it's important to remember one simple fact. *You have a choice. You can choose to do it, or you can choose not to do it.* Whether you go through with a public appearance depends only on how badly you want it and what feelings you're willing to work through to do it. By using the Vocal Awareness method, you're creating a scaffold to support the ongoing process of constructing your Self.

The same holds true for any step you take: You need to acknowledge your feelings about the projected consequences while at the same time provide yourself with a means to cope with them. For instance, maybe you'll no longer allow yourself to look away or giggle inappropriately, but instead you'll replace that avoidance behavior with consciously allowing a deep and loving breath and reminding yourself to release any tension that you're holding in your jaw. Or perhaps you'll simply say a phrase to yourself, such as "It's okay to *Take My Time.* I'm going to enjoy myself."

Perhaps, at first, you're likely to find yourself implementing the Vocal Awareness techniques in small increments and with occasional resistance. But as you conscientiously practice your daily vocal work-outs and persist in consciously revealing your

Voice—your identity—in the world, the System you're about to learn will bring you confidence and you'll gain momentum. It is a pragmatic way of working to manifest your personal vision of how you want your life to be and how you want to convey it.

Your Life—The Hero's Journey

There is a common misunderstanding about the nature of the hero's journey. Ancient myths and legends often emphasize an ultimate victory, such as Perseus cutting off the head of the evil Medusa, St. George killing the dragon, or Judith slaying the Assyrian general Holofernes. But that's not what the hero's journey is actually about. It is about the journey. It is about the multitude of small victories and discoveries along the way that it takes to get to the final one. That one could not exist without the others. If you stumble off the path and lose your way, you will never arrive at your ultimate destination.

History holds many examples of true heroism from where we can study and draw knowledge, such as the 1914 expedition led by explorer Sir Ernest Shackleton intended to make the first crossing on foot of the Antarctic continent. He and his 27 men got within 85 miles of their goal when their ship, so aptly named *Endurance*, foundered in the ice. In her book *The*

Endurance, historian Caroline Alexander describes their 20-month ordeal and two near-fatal attempts they made to escape by open boat before their final rescue. Remarkably, not a single life was lost in spite of storms; the cold; fear and uncertainty; emotional stress; and a shortage of food, water, and other supplies. This is astonishing, considering that of the three small boats on which Shackleton's men survived, the largest, the *James Caird*, was only 22-½ feet long, while they faced 60-foot waves and 80 mph winds as they traveled through 800 miles of the most treacherous ocean in the world.

How did the crew survive? From the beginning, Sir Ernest paid meticulous attention to detail and maintained a structure of command and the ship's routine. His heroism as a responsible leader enabled the group to survive their circumstances. He knew how to speak to each of his men, not only in words, but also in deeds, in a way he knew they could *hear* him. He did what needed to be done day in and day out. As Alexander writes:

> Behind every calculated word and gesture lay the single-minded determination to do what was best for his men. At the core of Shackleton's gift for leadership in crisis was an adamantine conviction that quite ordinary individuals were capable of heroic feats if the circumstances required; the weak and the strong could and must survive together. The

mystique that Shackleton acquired as a leader may partly be attributed to the fact that he elicited from his men strength and endurance they had never imagined they possessed; he ennobled them.[1]

During World War II, singer Josephine Baker worked as a spy for the French underground. Because of her high profile and popularity as an entertainer—a diva—she was able to travel openly with an entourage whose identities the Nazi Germans never questioned. Thus, she frequently smuggled people in and out of different European countries. Within and around her musical arrangements, she also scribbled notations that were actually codes and instructions for the Resistance. Her life was heroic.

One of the challenges we face in the modern world is that we no longer consider our lives heroic. We think we're just "going to work" everyday. Unfortunately, that's an uninspired attitude. There can be profound satisfaction in doing any job well. But even if you do not believe your job is significant enough to matter, you can choose to live and work at it from a higher vision. Whether you are a boss or an assistant, you can *inspire* the people around you and imbue their lives—and yours—with meaning.

Yes, the act of revealing yourself in public can seem intimidating. It may feel risky and exposing. But the rewards of committing to your expression can be

---

[1] Caroline Alexander, *The Endurance: Shackleton's Legendary Antarctic Expedition.* New York: Alfred A. Knopf, 1999.

phenomenal for you—and for those around you. There's a payoff! A good example of someone who focused his attention on being his best, instead of any potential obstacles or fears, occurred several years ago at the end of a five-day workshop I was leading at the Esalen Institute, a retreat center located in Big Sur, California. Twenty participants were there, including two longtime students of mine, a woman named Sherry and her brother Dean, a 35-year-old man with Down's syndrome. We were using the Big Yurt, a rotunda-like structure, for a closing ceremony. The space was more intimidating than most because the acoustics from the center made your voice echo and sound as though it was the "voice of God."

During our closing ceremony, the participants shared an expression of their newfound Vocal Awareness: a story, a poem, or a song. Everyone stood at the back of the room to deliver theirs, except for Dean. When his turn came, he looked up so he could locate the exact center of the rotunda—and step into it. He then sang "Kumbaya" at a performance level. Because he gave us the gift of his fullest expression of Self in that moment, his song was deeply moving and inspirational. He ennobled us and encouraged us to strive even more.

Dean was a young man totally committed to not hiding. If he had stood in the rear and not claimed the space or had he held back his Voice, none of us would have had the extraordinary experience in his presence that we did. So, as you can see, Self-acceptance, and the willingness to be revealed as the person you are, is a key to becoming free and a key to achieving Vocal Power.

Do you recall my student Matt Fong from the last chapter? He was so committed to a 30-minute speech he was giving—he was determined to impart his message and have an impact—that we did at least five hours of sessions together in preparation, and he practiced his text using the Vocal Awareness techniques for another ten to 15 hours on his own. He called me after his presentation and his spirits were soaring. He had done the entire speech without using any notes and it was tremendously well received! Matt is heroic in his approach to his personal mission, which is to serve the public good.

Taking the Next Step

You have already learned that perception is reality, and you can decide how you want to be perceived. Now you also understand that your current vocal and communication challenges are likely to be protective habits that you acquired in the past. And just as heroes must courageously and mindfully travel each step on their paths, they also have to be prepared and empower themselves to deal with whatever comes up along the journey. Until now, you may not have realized that you had a veritable treasure chest of vocal and presentational tools to draw upon. But get ready. By using the Vocal Awareness method, you're about to open the lid—peek inside—and reap the riches from within!

In the next two chapters, you will learn the Vocal Awareness techniques that will enable you to be more comfortable and confident in revealing while revealing your Self. You will also discover how to integrate your Voice and your life through the transformative process of the Vocal Awareness method.

Learning the Fundamental Techniques

Creation requires an uncommon mind and strong will serving an original view of life and the world.

—Jacques Barzun

We have already discussed the nature of Vocal Power and the most common vocal and communication challenges. Now it is time to get practical and learn the steps that can help you claim ownership of your Voice—with a capital V—on every level. In this chapter, I am going to teach you the fundamental techniques of Vocal Awareness. Among them are seven empowerment rituals to be used concurrently with the exercises you'll learn in Chapter 4, "The Daily Vocal Workout." By the way, when I use the word "ritual," I am not referring to a candle lighting ceremony but rather to a sequential procedure that will be purposefully repeated in the Work to deepen your focus.

It is very important that you don't skip ahead even if you don't quite grasp the merits of this phase of the Work yet. If you stick with me and follow through diligently and patiently on the fundamentals I'm teaching here, I guarantee you that these principles will become your anchor for Vocal Power. These rituals alone can transform you, your Voice, and your life. But you must give yourself the opportunity to learn them and integrate them.

Learning the Fundamentals

Just as you need a solid foundation to build a strong house, you likewise need a solid foundation to build a strong Voice. So, it is important to take your time and learn how to perform the Vocal Awareness techniques properly and effectively. The structure of the techniques (and the daily workout that builds upon them) is particular; you must adhere to its guidelines in order to reap the greatest rewards. It is likely to take several sessions to integrate all of the instructions you're about to receive. But once you do, you will find the structure liberating rather than constricting.

Freedom without direction is chaos.
As we provide direction, we have the
opportunity for creating life on our own terms.

Please also keep this in mind: Although the structure of the Vocal Awareness method is absolute, it is also straightforward and purposefully simple. In fact, there is only one correct way to perform each part of the workout, just as in ballet where there's only one proper way to stand in first position. So if you ever find yourself doing something that seems complicated or are feeling confused, that's your cue to hold a dialogue with your Self and return to the fundamentals.

We'll talk about dialoguing later. For now, review and practice these instructions as many times as you need to at the most basic level until they are ingrained in your mind/body/spirit. Always follow the motto KISS, which stands for:

Keep
It
Simple
Sweetheart

Be Respectful and Compassionate

Imagine what you would do in a dojo, a martial arts studio, before you were about to engage in a contest. You would bow. Why? Out of respect. Likewise, you must conduct your vocal workout with honor, respect, and compassion. Please trust me. I am not overstating this. However, in case I am making this seem a bit daunting, I should also point out that practicing these vocal techniques is a joyful experience. It will be exhilarating as you discover your Voice and gain a new freedom of expression.

It is important to develop your voice as though you are raising an infant. Every seemingly insignificant discovery is a milestone. Look, he rolled over! Look, she sat up! These are exciting events because they never happened before. You wouldn't compare your 11-month-old to the neighbor's child. You wouldn't care if someone else's baby took a step before yours did. Or you wouldn't run home and tell your baby: "Hurry up, you're not developing fast enough!" Would you? No. So, don't treat yourself like that either. Instead, give up your judgments and be supportive of your process. Be joyful.

Finding Your Stance

The first thing you need to do before you can begin making sound, or vocalizing, is to identify the appropriate stance or posture in which to work. One of the best ways to learn this is by playing around with various positions until you find the correct one. As you'll soon discover, the body has an innate intelligence and muscular memory. On a subconscious level, it retains information and even responds to the commands you give it. Granted some people are more in touch with their kinesthetic awareness than others. But everyone can become more conscious. With practice, it becomes easier to sense when you have shifted out of position and when to make the necessary adjustments.

The Vocal Awareness method is nonexclusionary. It can be performed seated just as well as it can be performed standing. If you choose or need to remain in your chair, simply follow the instructions skipping any indications to stand and then sit.

Are you ready to play? Okay, try a brief exploration in front of a mirror. (For now, a mirror is the only tool you'll need.) Stand up now if you plan to work on your feet. Otherwise, begin from your current position.

Without making any physical adjustments, notice your body language. Scan from your toes to the tip of your head and along your arms. Take in the whole picture. Don't change a thing as you get you feel settled. How does that feel?

Now, stand or sit in *stature* as though extraordinary about yourself. I don't ask that you believe it—yet. Just do it. Notice the difference. Does the room seem any quieter? Do you feel any different inside? Can you recall the first thing your body did when you gave it the command: "Stand in stature" or "Sit in stature"? Observe that the body's response is to inhale.

Now, stand or sit at attention. What does it feel like? Did you breathe? No. This is not the correct posture for your vocal workout because the chest has lifted and your shoulder and abdominal muscles have become tense and constricted.

Then, stand or sit in stature again. Imagine a string gently pulling you up through the top of your head. Reflect a wonderful Self-admiring person. Standing or sitting in stature is not only a physical posture but also a state of mind and feeling.

I realize it may take awhile to feel as though you inhabit the posture. But do it anyway—even if you don't fully understand and/or feel resistance doing it. In my teens and early 20s, I had very low Self-esteem, and standing in stature seemed almost fraudulent. Then I started building my own "public relations" and an internal shift resulted. This posture is completely natural and appropriate. Stature is one of the ways you can practice your commitment to the persona statement you wrote in Chapter 1.

In a posture of stature, your head should be erect, your shoulders level, and your legs should be about a foot apart. You should breathe naturally. If you are seated, your feet should be flat on the floor. It is important to be able to breathe freely and deeply in this stance and to feel a solid connection to the ground. Experiment by separating your legs to a greater distance. Then, place your feet together. Turn your toes straight ahead, then in, and then out. In which stature do you feel best, most confident? Some people find that putting one foot slightly forward as they stand actually helps create more space to breathe within the abdomen.

We'll discuss the importance of body language more in Chapter 6.

The Jaw Release

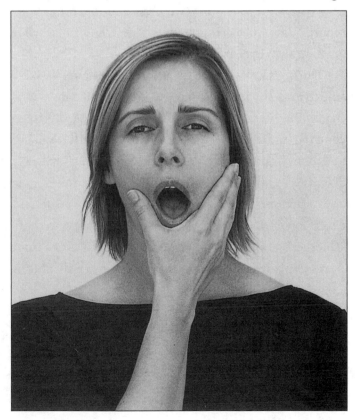

Once you are standing or sitting in stature, you are ready to learn how to perform the physical and sound making dynamics of the vocal workout. The Jaw Release is a component of most of the Vocal Awareness exercises I am about to describe. It helps to eliminate any tension you may be holding in your tongue, jaw muscles, and temporal mandibular joints. You can locate the temporal mandibular joints by placing your fingertips in front of your ears and opening your mouth. The correct spot is where you feel a space opening up as your jawbones move.

During the Jaw Release, your initial aim is to be able to extend your mouth open enough that you can fit three fingers stacked one on top of the other between your top and bottom rows of teeth. You will be using one hand—positioned in a specific way that I'll describe in a moment—to stretch your lower jaw downward gently and persuasively. Even so, you should never force your jaw open. If at first you can only achieve a one-finger or two-finger extension, work from there. Over time, your jaw will become more flexible as a result of practicing the vocal workout.

The Vocal Awareness method can offer you relief from the condition known as temporomandibular joint syndrome ("TMJ"). TMJ will be discussed at length in Chapter 5. Many people experience this common disorder, which can be painful and makes it difficult to

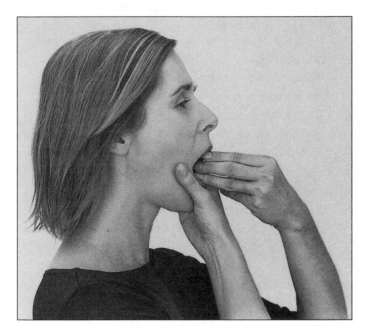

extend the jaw fully. If you ever tend to grind your teeth, clutch your jaw, or hear a popping sound when you chew, these are signs that you may have unresolved stress and TMJ. Please remember to be gentle whenever you work especially in this case.

To perform the Jaw Release properly and effectively, form a "V" with your hand by spreading your thumb away from your forefinger. Rest your hand against the ledge of your chin, just below your mouth, with your thumb on one side of your jaw and your fingers against the other. Your chin will be in the exact center of the "V." Experiment with different hand positions so you can discover for yourself the specificity of this position. Raise your hand position an eighth of an inch. Lower it an eighth of an inch. Shift it slightly to the right and to the left. Then, bring it back to center. Doesn't this feel more secure? That's why the right position is not arbitrary.

Now, use gentle pressure to ease your jaw downwards until your mouth is open, released, and as comfortable as possible. Remember not to force the extension. Simply use the weight of your hand as a pulley. Then, relax. Keep breathing as deeply and lovingly as possible as you hold this position.

Check your mirror to see whether you are doing the technique correctly. Your tongue should be resting easily, lightly touching your lower teeth. Your head should be level. You never want it to drop or rise as you release your jaw. The aim is to experience a complete lack of tension in your jaw. So give yourself a mental reminder to let go of any feeling of holding you may have. Your jaw should be loose and hang freely.

> All tension is fear-based.
> Where there is fear, there is doubt.
> Where there is doubt, there is no divinity.

With practice, you'll find it quite easy to achieve a feeling of complete release. As a result, you'll experience a new freedom in your sound making, which in turn will lead to a more open and easy style of communication. Furthermore, since tension depletes energy, you'll have more energy after doing the Jaw Release.

The Seven Empowerment Rituals

In the preceding chapters, I have made the point that the Vocal Awareness method is unique and produces exceptional results because it liberates and enhances the combined. power of your mind/body/spirit. Basically, it helps you focus your mind and cultivate greater Self-awareness. It strengthens and stretches the muscles involved in breathing and sound making. At the same time, it also enables you to grow and flourish emotionally and spiritually. The empowerment rituals make these developments possible. Without them, the System would not be complete or as personally transformational as it is.

I have found that professional athletes tend to grasp the importance of the empowerment rituals very quickly. When I worked with basketball superstar Earvin "Magic" Johnson, we did a role-playing activity. First, I had him walk into the room as he would walk onto the basketball court during a regular season game and then as he would walk in for a championship game. There was a notable change in his stature, eyes, and intensity. I asked him to describe the difference. He said, "Day-to-day, there's a lot going on in my mind. But during a championship, I have one focus." Right away, he saw that the Vocal Awareness rituals are designed to create a comparable focus that would support his Voice. The empowerment rituals help us achieve excellence.

The empowerment rituals are the internal processes that will take place within your mind's eye—your conscious awareness—as you vocalize and perform the biomechanical activities of the vocal workout. They are an important technique for cultivating your mind/body/spirit for two major reasons. First, they teach you to surrender to the process. Second, they help make the Work more complete. The fourth ritual, for example, makes sound visual. When you perceive sound vibrations, which are invisible to the naked eye, as traveling through an endless arc from your body through and beyond any destination, your communication has much greater clarity and impact. Imaging sound is a vital piece of this Work.

Now, we're going to discover the empowerment rituals one at a time.

Ritual 1:
Thank You to My Source

As I mentioned in Chapter 1, surrender is an exceedingly important principle of Vocal Awareness and of life in general. Surrendering allows us to serve the Work even when, in fact, we may be afraid to take the risk required for our success, or we feel resistant because we're tired, or we are just having a bad day. By requiring and allowing ourselves to do the Work, through surrendering to something greater than ourselves, we encourage ourselves to become more whole and more connected. Even when we're afraid, and despite any momentary concerns, we won't stop ourselves because we recognize that we are serving something more powerful than the ego-centered Self, something bigger than merely "me."

What exactly does thanking the Source mean? It depends on the individual. For many people this first ritual involves offering a simple "thank you" to God. But what if you are an atheist or an agnostic and don't believe in God? Then perhaps you will take this opportunity to thank your parents. But what if you don't like your parents? In that case, consider a slightly deeper perspective: someone deserves to be thanked because someone created you. You can use the ritual moment of *Thank You to My Source* simply to reflect on your gratitude for the moment of creation when you came into being. This attitude will help you develop adherence to the concept of surrender.

Ritual 2:
Love and Let Go

Gratitude and surrender should not only extend outwards as a way of honoring a natural power or deity greater than us. We must also acknowledge ourselves for showing up and participating as fully as we can in the Work. By practicing this second ritual, we show ourselves respect and acceptance. The body responds with gratitude and surrender. You can always tell when it does because it will instinctively breathe.

To understand this ritual thoroughly, I want you to do a brief experiment similar to the one you did when you learned what it feels like to stand in stature. My students use this method in all my workshops, and it is very effective.

Now, sit down and relax. Just kick back and let all your tension go. Get comfy. Then, notice how you sat down. Did you slump in your chair? Did you cross your legs? Notice how you feel when you are relaxed. Also notice how the space around you feels. Got it? Then, please stand again.

All I ask is that you "turn off" your left-brain, the hemisphere that rules reasoning and logic. Don't try to understand this intellectually before you have the experience. Don't think about "what" or "why." Then, when you're ready, sit down once more and merely hear the words inside your mind: *Love and Let Go*. Imagine what this might feel like. Don't try to figure it out. Take a moment to absorb the experience. Let it filter down through the conscious mind into your muscle and sense memory. Observe. And when you choose to, stand again. Notice: Do either you or the room feel any different now? Does the room seem quieter or stiller? Are you more centered?

In retrospect, what was the first thing your body did when asked to *Love and Let Go*? Did you notice that it inhaled? I teach throughout the world. It doesn't matter whether the phrase is translated into Japanese or German. In all walks of life, the body always does the same thing when asked to *Love and Let Go*. It breathes. It is your body's way of saying, "Thank you for the permission to be my Self. I'll breathe in acknowledgment."

The phrase *Love and Let Go* will come to hold a very personal meaning for you. Love may mean experiencing your connections to your fellow beings and loved ones. For me, the word "love" gives me permission to be the best I can be and acknowledges the creative force within me. When I focus on it, my attitude becomes more open and receptive. To do this requires courage, dedication, and vigilance.

Consider this ritual as an opportunity to show your willingness to receive and share. Letting go may represent freedom from fear, tension, and whatever else holds you back or blocks your personal progress and growth. With this ritual, you can let go of heavy emotional baggage and judgments. You can accept and surrender to the vision of your persona statement from Chapter 1 instantaneously. Even if you are unaware of the cognitive connection, your body language will shift and you'll inhale.

> Power develops out of freedom,
> freedom out of letting go,
> and letting go out of knowledge.

RITUAL 3:
Allow a Silent, Loving, Down-through-my-body Breath

Vocal Awareness begins with an awareness of breath, for the breath is the source of all sound and the connective vibration of life. Breathing calms and energizes the body. It is also emotionally expansive and liberating. With this third ritual, we'll take ourselves one step deeper into conscious communion with life.

In order to identify the feeling of this ritual breath, I would like you to do another experiment to heighten your kinesthetic awareness. Begin by standing or sitting comfortably in stature, erect and relaxed with a certain sense of dignity. Refrain from judging the process. Take a deep breath, as though it's the "top of the morning" and great to be alive. Notice how it feels to inhale like this. Then, exhale and relax.

Now, I want you to experience a different kind of a breath. This time, allow your mind/body/spirit to respond to these specific thoughts during successive breaths:

- ♪ *Allow a silent breath.* Now exhale. Notice the difference from the breath you first "took." With your first breath, didn't your chest rise and your abdomen constrict? When you "allowed" a breath, your abdomen and rib cage both expanded. It was much simpler and more relaxed.

- ♪ *Allow a silent and loving breath.* Now exhale. How was that different? The body responds to emotions. In a trauma, we hold the breath and shut down feeling. When we breathe lovingly, we do the opposite.

- ♪ *Allow a Silent, Loving, Down-through-my-body Breath.* Now exhale. Again, take time to observe what changed and how you felt. That should have been magnificent and pleasurable. In fact, do it once more and really enjoy the experience.

The subtle differences you notice here can lead to a profound change in your Voice. By learning to be in your breath, you are learning to be in your Self—and in the moment. Always take at least six to eight counts to feel the breath flow through your mouth or nose and down through your body before releasing it.

From now on, you will use the first three rituals prior to making sound. They will serve to separate you from one reality and establish you in another. Use them to shift gears from what you were doing to a more open and receptive state of readiness. They will also increase your ability to focus on what you are doing. The remaining four rituals will be employed as sound is being made. That means every single time you make sound and in every single exercise. Remember: *Never skip the rituals.*

RITUAL 4:
See the Nasal Edge and Arc of Sound

You are now going to add sound to the exhalation of your breath. At present, while you are learning the dynamics of the empowerment rituals, you will simply hum through gently closed lips: *Hmm.* Later, when you get to the vocal workout (in Chapter 4), different physical activities, vowel sounds, and spoken words will be added to the program. Hums are always appropriate. Be sure that you are positioned in front of a mirror.

Begin by taking a few moments to practice the Jaw Release that you learned earlier in this chapter. It is important that you release any tension that you may be holding in your tongue, jaw, neck, and shoulders. One of the most common trouble areas is the tongue. Not only does it seem to have a mind of its own, but it's also the strongest muscle, per diameter, in the body. Sometimes it seems as if the tongue has grown enormously in size and practically needs a straitjacket to control it. It grabs, pulls, and dances uncontrollably. Our job is to teach the tongue what to do. Use this opportunity to become sensitized to what it's like to neutralize your tongue. Allow it to let go and release, laying forward in your mouth, resting comfortably against your bottom teeth—doing absolutely nothing.

When you feel that your tension has been sufficiently released, drop your hand from your jaw and gently close your lips. Before you hum—or make any sound during the vocal workout—perform the first three rituals:

1. Thank You to My Source;
2. Love and Let Go;
3. Allow a Silent, Loving, Down-through-my-body Breath.

Then, initiate the sound, which in this case is *Hmm*, on the exhalation.

Go through this process two or three times now to coordinate your breath with the sound. Exhale lovingly and expressively for a lingering count of approximately six to eight beats.

Now, put a finger right under your nose. Do a hum. Notice everything you can about it. Then, lower your finger about an eighth of an inch and align your fingernail with the edge of your top lip. This focal point is called the "Nasal Edge." Whenever you

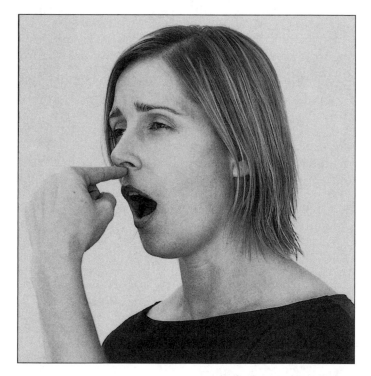

Incorrect position: Nasal Edge

vocalize, focus on projecting sound "forward" through and out of this special spot. From now on, this should be your mental anchor.

Keeping your finger in position, practice two or three more hums and see if you can feel the vibration here. Make your humming sound extremely nasal. Experiment with different pitches, or notes, until you find one that is comfortably within your vocal range. By vocal range, I mean it is neither too high nor too low to sustain for six to eight counts with consistent energy. Observe how the sound differed just from making a subtle adjustment of an eighth of an inch with your finger.

Okay, we're halfway there.

Now, tilt your finger and your hand upward at about a 45-degree angle and picture a line extending beyond them. Do not tilt your head, and do not tighten your neck and shoulders. What you are creating is a leaping off point for your sound. Practice nasal humming again with your hand in this position, and follow the sound along this trajectory. See the sound emanating "forward," flying right out off the Nasal Edge. Notice, again, that it sounds a little different now.

The Nasal Edge is a "sweet spot," like the place on a tennis racquet where ball and racquet interconnect effortlessly as the ball hits the racquet squarely. Using

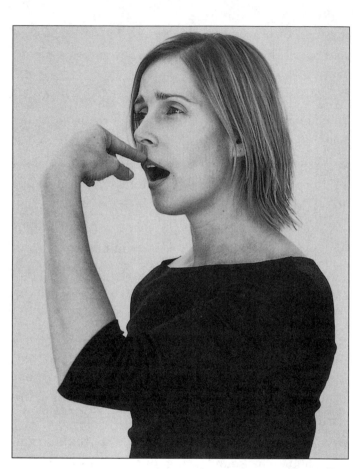

Correct position: Nasal Edge

this mental image will significantly enhance your ability to project your vocal and personal energy with confidence. This begins to make sound visual.

Let's add the concept of the Arc of Sound. The principle behind it is called the "Bernoulli effect." The

Bernoulli effect states that a gas or liquid in motion will exert less than normal pressure upon its surrounding environment. This effect is the reason that an airplane can take off. As the plane moves forward, the air that passes over its wings exerts less pressure, so the plane lifts. Your breath also lifts as it leaves your body.

Here is an easy experiment you can do that illustrates the workings of this principle. Hold a piece of paper just beneath your bottom lip and blow across the top of the paper. The paper will rise because the air pressure above it is reduced by the motion of the air. And the pressure beneath the paper is then sufficient to lift the paper. The Bernoulli effect explains all aerodynamic phenomena from throwing a ball to ski jumping to playing a clarinet to singing.

While speaking or singing, the vocal folds vibrate because air passes through them. During this vibratory cycle, the vocal folds are drawn together and sound is created, and as the breath (pressure flow) continues, the air passage narrows sufficiently so that the Bernoulli effect is created. Therefore, I have designed the exercises in the vocal workout to increase your airflow and intensify the pressure from your lungs to strengthen your vocal muscles. For a similar reason, I am also going to ask you to train your mind's eye to "see" your Voice moving through an Arc of Sound.

The Arc of Sound is the most powerful image you can use to enhance your vocal production. When you inhale fully and deeply, energy in the power of your breath wells up inside of you. Then, as sound emerges from your body along a 45-degree angle, you can let it soar up and outwards like a ski jumper taking off from a ramp.

Eventually, it will descend on its own. Gravity will bring it down. But you do not have to focus on the descent, only on the upward trajectory. Focus on the sound moving through and beyond the arc as you

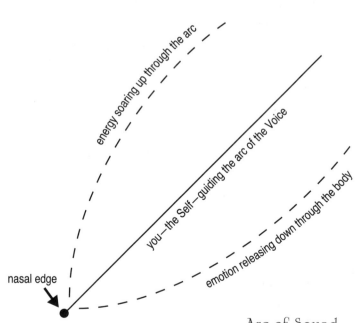

Arc of Sound

would if you were throwing a ball. That simple follow-through can make a world of difference.

Here's the experience I'm asking you to explore: As the sound soars upward, allow your emotions to move downward through your body simultaneously. Sense the expansion and fullness this creates, even as you are enabling free yet focused sound expression to ride the crest of the irresistible breath as though it is gliding through the air on a magic carpet ride.

Return now to your humming exercise. I want you to modify the pitch this time so that it begins higher and descends a few notes during your exhalation. Try a few hums with your fingernail resting on the Nasal Edge with your finger and hand tilted upward again. Then, you can let your arm drop and try a few more. Are you ready?

Remember to use the four rituals you have already learned:

♪ Thank You to My Source;

♪ Love and Let Go;

♪ Allow a Silent, Loving, Down-through-my-body Breath;

♪ See the Nasal Edge and Arc of Sound.

Stand or sit in stature. Begin inhaling. Check in your mirror again to ensure that your head remains level. Now, on the exhalation hum, *Hmm*, see the sound soar upward and outward through the Arc. Allow the pitch to descend slightly as you sustain the tone for six to eight counts. The sound should be extremely nasal.

Quite often, changing pitches challenges people. If you are having trouble, don't worry—just explore the biomechanics. Later on, as you become more fluid and comfortable with the process—perhaps as by exploring singing in Chapter 8—you can focus on going higher and lower or on finding the right notes.

Right now, simply take a moment to observe how you feel and what the sound you made was like before moving on to the next ritual.

Ritual 5:
Pay Attention/Deeper Listening

As you practice Vocal Awareness, you will be learning to use not only your outer ears but also your deep inner senses to *Pay Attention* to the process. When you explore your Voice, you explore your own power and mastery because the Voice is a metaphor for the integration of mind/body/spirit. Sound is both energy and emotion as it traverses the body. The body is a fluid system and is not isolated, as you may once have believed, from mind and feelings. In Vocal Awareness, we are always mindful of moving toward a deeper integration of ourselves.

In part, the journey to Vocal Power is a journey to develop a heightened level of focus. So, *Pay Attention/-Deeper Listening* should be enacted in every moment of the Work. A synonym for this concept in the language of Vocal Power is "conscious awareness." Observe and take notice of the subtle qualities of your sound, your body, your mind, your emotions, and your spirit.

Pay meticulous attention to details of the process, as this will increase your effectiveness. Listen for the messages of your inner Voice. The purpose of this System is to put you in contact with your deeper Self so that you gain empowerment. This ritual is your tool for focusing and becoming the very best Self you can be.

Ritual 6:
Take My Time

Don't hurry the Work. Determine the pace that best supports your journey. What counts is not speed but effectiveness. I'll talk more about this principle at the end of Chapter 4 in the section called "Designing Your Daily Practice." Suffice it to say that as you develop more awareness, you will discover your strengths and weaknesses and the areas of Voice on which you most need to focus. These may even change from day to day. Adhering to the structure of the Vocal Awareness method and taking the time you need to explore a particular exercise or principle is the way you will garner the greatest benefits. Giving your Self permission to take your time also cultivates an atmosphere of security.

Be less self-conscious and become more conscious of Self.

RITUAL 7:
Be Conscious of Self

Trust that if the present moment is all it can be, then the result will be what it needs to be. So be aware of the nuances of your physical and emotional experience. With practice, you'll find that a new fullness and Self-knowledge will begin to come through on every level. The Vocal Awareness method is leading you toward this ritual.

Please do not confuse greater awareness with being self-conscious in the derogatory sense of the term. Voice work is meant to bring you pleasure, not make you feel uncomfortable or behave awkwardly. Vocally powerful individuals are at ease within and project their Self-acceptance into the world. Self-conscious people, on the other hand, are cautious and tentative.

Remember: Your Voice is your identity. Conscious awareness of Self puts you in charge of how you are perceived, which will make you more comfortable when you are under pressure and need to be your best.

In addition to the pleasure you can derive both from being your best and from consciously choosing to develop your abilities, speaking and singing can feel and sound wonderful. So seek joy in your *conscious* breath, in the vibrations of sound resonating through your body, in the tones that please your ears, and the freedom of Self-expression. Do more of whatever feels good, and if it doesn't, don't do it.

Be conscious of your joyful Self.

Caution creates anxiety. Consciousness creates awareness.

Taking the Next Step

Now that you have learned the empowerment rituals—the internal processes of the Vocal Awareness method—you are ready to learn their biomechanical elements. Always remember: Whenever you perform the activities of the daily vocal workout (which you'll learn in the next chapter), you should apply the rituals simultaneously using the following checklist. Always have your Checklist at your side when doing activities:

The Vocal Awareness Checklist

♪ Thank You to My Source;

♪ Love and Let Go;

♪ Allow a Silent, Loving, Down-through-my-body Breath;

♪ See the Nasal Edge and Arc of Sound;

♪ Pay Attention/Deeper Listening;

♪ Take My Time;

♪ Be Conscious of Self.

The Daily Vocal Workout

Whatever you do, or dream you can do, begin.
Boldness has genius, power, and magic in it. Begin it now.
—Johann Wolfgang von Goethe

So far, you have gained a basic understanding of the Vocal Awareness method and some of the communication challenges it will resolve. We've discussed how each of us is an integrated mind/body/spirit system and explored the fundamental techniques that are the bedrock of the path to Vocal Power—standing or sitting in stature, the Jaw Release, and the empowerment rituals (a.k.a. the Vocal Awareness Checklist). In this chapter, I am going to teach you a series of five basic exercises using sound and breath. Then I'll outline a seven-minute daily practice routine and offer you a couple of success tips.

During your first few sessions, while you are learning how to do these techniques properly and effectively, you should proceed slowly, deliberately, and consciously. Take time to stop and reflect on the physical sensations you feel as well as your emotions and attitude. (You'll come to discover that's a good life strategy, too.) Soon, the logic and elegance of the program will become apparent. The Vocal Awareness method is more than a theory—it is a direct experience. You actually need to do it to understand and achieve the benefits fully.

Once you have learned this basic vocal workout, I encourage you to practice it first thing in the morning everyday. If you don't do so, there's a chance that you'll never get to it. You are forming a new behavioral habit and this requires a strong commitment. In a sense, this process is not unlike going on a diet. One reason that weight loss centers are such profitable businesses is that most of us lose and gain back the same ten pounds over and over again. To lose weight, we've actually got to stick to the plan. So, please commit to doing the vocal workout for a minimum of seven minutes for seven days. Then, renew your commitment for another week, then another, and so on.

Later, when doing your vocal workout has become an ingrained behavior, you can decide whether it fits better somewhere else in your daily schedule. Personally, I get up at 4 A.M. to pray and meditate, after which I go to the gym. Following the gym, my wife and I take a long walk together for about an hour and a half, and then I practice my Vocal Awareness techniques before I go to my studio.

My average workday includes 10 to 14 hours of session time. This means I have to go to bed a little earlier than I would otherwise; however, I always know that I will get my daily practices accomplished. It took many years to balance my schedule. Although I have a different schedule on the road, I still maintain the structure of my day.

Also, use the vocal workout prior to "performance" situations, such as important meetings, job interviews, telephone conferences or sales calls, presentations, speeches, lectures, on-air appearances, and singing, as well as before social encounters. You'll find that these techniques will shift and anchor your focus in as little as a minute, 30 seconds, or even a single breath. Make a detour to the restroom for a few moments if there's nowhere else to go to get some privacy. The more often you consciously prepare your voice with these warm-up techniques, the more deeply ingrained your Vocal Awareness will become in your mind/body/spirit.

PREPARING FOR A VOCAL WORKOUT: Gathering Tools

For the purpose of hygiene, please wash your hands before you begin. You will be placing your fingers in your mouth. In addition to your hands and fingers,

there are only a few items that you need to gather in order to do a successful vocal workout:

- ♪ A mirror: so that you can observe yourself,
- ♪ A washcloth or handkerchief: a tool for the first exercise,
- ♪ A pencil: a tool for the fourth exercise,
- ♪ A tape recorder: so that you can listen to your vocal workout and gain objective feedback,
- ♪ A video camera (optional): so you can both watch and listen to your vocal workout and gain feedback,
- ♪ The Vocal Awareness Checklist,
- ♪ A journal (optional): so you can record your observations and impressions.

If the idea of tape-recording or videotaping your workouts seems unappealing or even anxiety provoking to you, please understand that you must approach the process of developing Vocal Awareness with a nonjudgmental attitude. You need to take charge of creating a safe space to work and to be as respectful and compassionate of your emotional and spiritual needs as you would those of your most beloved friend. Aim to cultivate an atmosphere of trust and acceptance whenever and wherever you practice.

Creating a Safe Space

You don't need much space to do a vocal workout—literally just enough to lean forward without bumping your head on the wall or a piece of furniture. However, you may want to ensure your privacy. There's no reason that you absolutely must be alone during the workout, so long as you are not being distracted or worrying that you are disturbing someone else. Consider your workout a sacred part of your daily routine, as meaningful as a morning prayer and as habitual as brushing your teeth. So if necessary, shut the door to the room you're in, take your phone off the hook and turn off your pager, ask your family or roommate to respect your desire for solitude, and grant yourself complete permission to develop and nurture your Voice within this sanctuary.

More than one student has shared concerns with me about being seen and heard doing their vocal workouts. Sometimes they feel embarrassed by the possibility of being exposed while making loud sounds that might seem strange to the average listener or putting their hands to their mouths in ways that could strike an observer as unattractive. I gently guide them to understand that these kinds of emotional responses are deeply connected to their sense of identity. Accepting and experiencing their feelings while doing the workout or in a "performance" situation is as much a part of the Vocal Awareness method as any other. By creating a space to work where they won't be interrupted, any form of shame can surface in safety and be healed. We'll talk more about personal identity, exposure, and other emotional issues in Chapter 7.

> Solitude gives birth to the original in us, to beauty unfamiliar and perilous, to poetry.
>
> Thomas Mann, *Death in Venice*

Another concern of some students is that they are afraid that they'll literally bother and disrupt their neighbors. This is a common concern for those who live in apartment buildings with paper-thin walls or spend a lot of time on the road in hotel rooms. Dick Butkus, the great all-pro linebacker for the Chicago Bears and a former client of mine, came up with an imaginative solution for this problem when he became a football analyst for CBS Sports. He did his vocal workouts in his hotel room at 4:30 A.M. with a pillow pressed lightly in front of his face to muffle the sound. It worked like a charm. As you can see, there's really no reason to make excuses or avoid the vocal workout.

Planning so that you have an appropriate space to do your vocal workout is an essential aspect of your commitment to the process. Some of my students rent rehearsal studios for this purpose—although usually for longer workouts than the basic seven minutes I'll be teaching you in this chapter. But you can also solve a space dilemma in many other ways that cost no money. When I was a poor, young voice student and had few places where I could go to sing and vocalize in solitude, I would practice outside in a park sometimes. I also discovered a beautiful little church that always kept its doors unlocked and I would often practice there in the hours around midnight. The ambiance of both environments contributed to the pleasure I took in those early sessions.

By the way, as far as I am concerned, practicing your vocal workout in a car doesn't count unless you completely pull over to the curb or park in a parking lot. Just stopping at a red light is far too distracting. You'll be cheating yourself unless you give your vocal workout your full attention. That being said, I should point out that I have done effective practices in seemingly odd locations. I coached two stars of a summer stock musical during a heat wave one year. Because we needed some shade and no other room was available, we hauled a piano into the ladies' restroom. It was quite a resonant space—sort of like singing in the shower—and we enjoyed a good session there. Many times I've walked down Eighth Avenue in New York City, vocalizing along the way.

> The journey is never outward, but always and only inward toward discovery of the deeper Self.

Remember: This is a more subtle process than doing jumping jacks or stomach crunches. The techniques you are about to learn are not calisthenics and should never be approached aggressively. Although you will be building strength in your vocal muscles, your emphasis should be placed on quality of expression, clarity, and ease—not on quantity or force. The ultimate goal is to become a 100 percent conscious and comfortable communicator—mentally, physically, and emotionally.

Are you ready? Then let's get to it!

THE VOCAL WORKOUT EXERCISES: The Three Aspects

The Three Aspects are the distinct phases of activity that form the framework of the vocal workout. Each aspect incorporates all the elements of Vocal Awareness in varying percentages. From now on, plan to use them in sequence as your preparation for every type of vocal performance. We can define a "performance" as any situation where you need to be at your best whether it be a routine activity that you formerly took for granted or a major presentation.

Specifically, the preparation sequence includes:

♪ *The First Aspect—The Warm-Up.* During the Warm-Up, 90 percent of your focus will be on your technique—that is, your mind/body/spirit awareness—and ten percent on aesthetics, or the beauty of the sound. Just as an athlete or dancer always does a series of stretches before activity, your Voice needs some gentle and/or vigorous preparation in order to do its best work without straining. This aspect could be called "How I do what I do."

♪ *The Second Aspect—The Bridge.* Here, 65 percent of your focus will be on your technique and 35 percent on aesthetic quality. It represents a transition period between Warm-Up and actual performance, since now you apply the Warm-Up techniques to your material (words or a song). This aspect could be described as "How I do what I do as it is applied to what I am doing."

♪ *The Third Aspect—The Performance.* Now, your focus will only be ten percent on your technique and 90 percent on aesthetics. Because you have integrated the techniques with your material in the Bridge, you do not need to engage your intellect as often. At this level of the vocal workout, you should be continuously aware, as though you are a tightrope walker. This is not an anxious attention but a relaxed presence that is both alert and spacious, which is why this aspect could simply be called "Doing what I am doing."

Once you have reached the Performance, whenever you want or need to, you may feel free to go back to the Bridge. It is perfectly all right to move back and forth between the second and third aspects of the vocal workout without having to start at the beginning again with the Warm-Up exercises. Your material could be a poem, a speech, a request for a promotion, or a declaration of love.

I'll go into more detail about these three phases of activity and how best to perform each as we arrive at them within the vocal workout itself. Right now, let's discuss a few biomechanical and sound making elements that you'll need to understand as you do the Work.

Basic Elements of Movement and Sound

You've already learned the internal processes that accompany the physical movements and sounds of the vocal workout. There are only a few more elements required.

The Basic Yawn-Sigh

The Basic Yawn-Sigh is the Jaw Release with sound added to it. It is the foundation of most of the exercises in the vocal workout. To perform it correctly, you'll place your hand in the "V" position and extend your jaw.

Then, follow the seven rituals on the Vocal Awareness Checklist, lovingly expressing an open *Hah* sound as in the word "hat" on your exhalation. Please use the same descending tone that you learned while humming to discover your Nasal Edge and the Arc of Sound. The *Hah* sound should always be extremely nasal and visually soaring even as it descends.

As you make sound, or vocalize, continue to release your lower jaw, without forcing it. More instructions will be provided for each specific exercise.

The Breath Precedes the Tone

Remember Eliza Doolittle in *My Fair Lady* practicing her "H" sound in an exercise that Henry

Higgins gave her? "Hurricanes hardly (H) ever happen." The aspirated "H" sound opens the throat and helps propel the sound freely outward on a magic carpet of air. Don't confuse this with the breathiness of Marilyn Monroe or a soap opera voice.

Try laughing for a moment (Ha Ha Ha). Did you hear how the "H" naturally preceded the tone? Using the breath in this manner gives your voice extra projection without straining your larynx. Make a note of the sensation. This principle should guide your exhalations throughout the vocal workout.

Abdominal Support

As you do your exercises, pull your lower abdominal muscles up and *through* your sound. Don't merely contract your stomach inward. Instead, pull it in and up. Practice this contraction for a moment. Place your hand on your stomach and feel what pulling in is like. Then feel what pulling upward and in is like. Notice the difference.

When you pull upward, do you notice how the lower abdominals work more effectively? This principle of abdominal support will enable you to sustain consistent energy when you are speaking or singing.

It is not accidental that ballet dancers, equestrians, golfers, and people who meditate recognize the importance of the same area in the body. There is an energy center approximately three inches below the navel, which is widely recognized as a balancing point for activity and focus. Abdominal support will help you access its power.

Precautions

If you feel any little irritations in your throat, such as tickles, scratches, or any kind of pain, your Voice is probably telling you that you're doing something wrong. Remember: The vocal workout should never ever hurt. Pause and identify what could be causing the irritation. Your tongue or jaw may be too tight. You may be breathing too fast or forcing the air out of you instead of encouraging and guiding it as you exhale. Your neck and shoulders may be tense. Any one of these things could injure your voice by inhibiting its natural freedom. Review the empowerment rituals on the Vocal Awareness Checklist to find ways to relax into the exercises. Then begin again.

A Final Reminder

- ♪ Ensure that your tools are handy,
- ♪ Always keep the Vocal Awareness Checklist visible,
- ♪ Always be in stature,

♪ Remember to breathe,

♪ Release your tension,

♪ At all times remain conscious of the rituals,

♪ Don't judge! Fire your inner critic.

Okay, now you're ready to begin the vocal workout. Have fun!

THE FIRST ASPECT:
The Warm-Up

The Vocal Awareness method is like a spider's web: The whole thing begins to unravel when you remove a single strand. That's why technical precision and attention to detail are so vital to the first aspect of the Vocal Workout. The web you are weaving by doing this Work is the integration of your mental focus, kinesthetic memory (muscular and sensory responses), your emotional state, and your spiritual intention. Here, your mind is focused intently on every part of what your body is doing. Focus always comes first!

Take your time and be conscientious. Nonetheless, don't merely warm up mechanically and please don't hear your vocalizations simply as sound. Rather, feel them as an emotional expression—an emotion based on love. Release your Self through the breath. Experience the sounds as sensually and aesthetically as possible.

Sound is expressed emotion.

Remember: The Warm-Up can be compared more accurately to a ballet dancer doing stretches at the barre than a fitness trainer doing an aerobics drill. That's because the desired outcome is beauty, strength, expression, and flexibility rather than merely strength alone. Often referred to as its "color" or "timbre," the tone of a sound *always* includes emotional qualities.

Use moderate vocal dynamics. By this, I mean a moderately soft to a moderately loud voice. Trained singers would call these dynamics "mezzo piano" (very soft) to "mezzo forte" (very loud). It is important not to work in extremes (e.g., very soft or very loud) until you can effectively control your voice.

You will perform four exercises in every Warm-Up; however, there is a substitute for the third one and you may alternate these two exercises from session to session. The sequence you'll follow is:

♪ The Tongue Pull,

♪ The Two-Finger Yawn-Sigh,

♪ The Hanging Yawn-Sigh or The Supported Yawn-Sigh,

♪ The Pencil Technique.

Warm-Up 1: The Tongue Pull

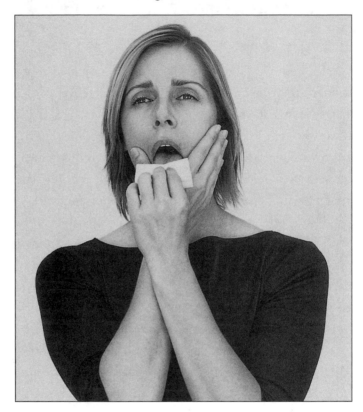

In this exercise, you will be using your washcloth or handkerchief to pull on your tongue gently as you do the Yawn-Sigh. Don't use tissue or paper toweling, because they'll stick to your tongue. The Tongue Pull allows you to experience an unobstructed and very free flow of sound and helps release tongue tension.

Begin by standing or sitting in stature. As you learned before, make a "V" with one hand and place it on your chin and jaw. Apply a gentle, downward pressure to ease your jaw open. Your mouth should be open to a length of about three fingers. Allow your tongue to rest against your bottom teeth. Keep your head level—you don't want it to drop forward as your jaw is released. Check your mirror to see that you're doing the technique correctly.

Now, gently take hold of your tongue with the cloth in your other hand. Pull your tongue down and out of your mouth, carefully and steadily. Do not yank on it or strain it, even as you pull it well out of your mouth. Your tongue should feel and look released, not bunched up, or tight. At first you may feel that your tongue wants to fight you or quivers with tension. Remember that you're in charge here. Simply keep pulling it gently downward. Check in your mirror again to ensure that your head remains level.

Now, do a Yawn-Sigh, while pulling your tongue, using the sound of *Hah* as in "hat." Allow the pitch to descend slightly as you simultaneously sustain the tone. See the sound soaring through the nasal edge and arc. The sound should be extremely nasal. Apply all the rituals on the Vocal Awareness Checklist.

Notice the remarkable sensation of stretching you feel. Optional: Record your impressions of your thoughts, physical sensations, and emotions in your Vocal Power journal. I'll discuss making observations at the end of this chapter in "Designing Your Daily Practice."

Nasality causes the greatest attenuation—tautness—in the laryngeal muscle and most efficient vibration within the vocal folds themselves. It also helps raise the soft palate while creating a mental focus toward the front of the hard palate. When you complete the exercise, the nasality therefore translates to enhanced resonance and an intellectual understanding of where to *feel* the sound always.

Please take note that we create these nasal sounds—without adding extra tension—only during the vocal workout. Never walk around singing or speaking nasally on purpose. If you have ever been told that you have a "nasal voice," don't worry. Using the nasality in the exercises will enhance the richness and character of your voice. (I realize this may seem like an oxymoron, but trust me.)

WARM-UP 2: The Two-Finger Yawn-Sigh

In this exercise, you will be inserting the index and middle fingers of one hand beneath your tongue as you do the Yawn-Sigh. This technique liberates tension in the tongue and mouth. It allows the soft palate to rise without you even thinking about it, thereby creating more space in your mouth. Of course, placing your fingers in your open mouth sometimes gets a little "juicy," but the benefits far outweigh any inconvenience.

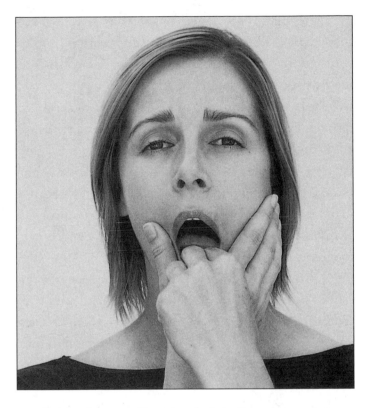

Begin by standing or sitting in stature. As you learned before, make a "V" with one hand and place it on your chin and jaw. Apply a gentle, downward pressure to ease your jaw open. Your mouth should be open to a length of about three fingers. Allow your tongue to rest gently against your bottom teeth. Keep your head level—you don't want it to drop forward as your jaw is released. Check your mirror to see that you're doing the technique correctly.

Now, place two fingers under your tongue—not too far back—allowing it to release forward on top of your fingers. Use your thumb of the same hand to gently press under your chin at the spot where you can feel the base of the tongue muscle in order to check for tension. First, practice simply tightening and releasing your tongue in this position so that you become familiar with the sensation when you're relaxed. Your tongue should feel soft and released. Tension will cause it to feel bunched up and hard. Check your mirror.

Now, do a Yawn-Sigh, with your fingers under your tongue, using the sound *Hah* as in "hat." Allow the pitch to descend slightly as you sustain the tone. See the sound soaring through the nasal edge and arc. The sound should be extremely nasal. Apply all the rituals on the Vocal Awareness Checklist. Continue releasing your jaw downward, persuading it with the hand on your jaw rather than pulling on your teeth. Beware of a tendency to spread your mouth or get tight—don't!

Notice the sensation of space that is created in your mouth. You'll be able to hear a richer, warmer tone in your voice almost immediately afterward. With practice, you'll gain a high degree of control over your tongue.

Optional: Record your impressions in your Vocal Power journal.

WARM-UP 3:
The Hanging Yawn-Sigh

In this exercise, you will be bending over at the waist as you do the Yawn-Sigh. This variation helps put you in touch with possible tensions in your upper body and neck that may interfere with good vocal production. It also enables your posture to correct itself. In addition, it is a good method to experience the principle of abdominal support.

Begin by standing in stature. Then, soften your knees slightly and drop your head forward. The knee bend helps protect your lower back. Keep gently rolling down, one vertebra at a time, until you are hanging limply forward from the waist. The top of your head should be pointing toward the floor. Your arms should be dangling freely from your shoulders— with the tips of your fingers at about the height of your shins. Notice that there may be a tendency to hold tension in the back of your neck. Allow your Self to breathe deeply and relax in this position.

This technique is best done standing. However, if you choose to do the Hanging Yawn-Sigh in a seated position, it is preferable to sit toward the front edge of your chair and place your feet, ankles, and knees close together so that your arms will have room to hang freely on either side of them. In this case, begin by sitting in stature, then drop your head forward and roll down through your spine until your head is above your knees and your arms are dangling freely from your shoulders. As above, in the directions for the standing variation, notice whether there is a tendency to hold tension, especially in the back of your neck. Allow your Self to breathe deeply and relax in this position.

Then, whether you are standing or seated, very slowly come back up. Imagine your Self gradually unwinding with the flexibility of a cat. Don't hold your breath—keep inhaling and exhaling. Your head should be the last part of you to return to the upright position. Practice the downward and upward motions until you're comfortable with them.

Now, bending over again, let go with your body as completely as possible. Let your arms drop toward the floor and release all tension in your body. Gently roll your head around, and then be still.

For those who experience chronic back pain, a third variation of the Hanging Yawn-Sigh is to hang your body over the arm or back of a sofa or the edge of a bed. Once you get situated in the hanging position, release your tension as best you can, but do not attempt to roll up and down through your spine.

Do a Yawn-Sigh in this hanging over position, using the sound of *Hah* as in "hat." Allow the pitch to descend slightly as you sustain the tone. See the sound soaring through the nasal edge and arc. Apply all the rituals on the Vocal Awareness Checklist.

When you're done, come up very slowly and rest.

Try a Two-Finger Yawn-Sigh, while standing or sitting upright, on the sound of *Hah.* Allow the pitch to descend slightly as you sustain the tone. Apply all the rituals on the Vocal Awareness Checklist. You may be surprised to discover that your voice has improved noticeably as a result of hanging over limply.

Now bend forward again, and support your jaw

with your hand in the "V" position you have been using while hanging limply. Do a Yawn-Sigh on the sound of *Hah* as you slowly roll up to an upright standing or seated position—taking a full six to eight counts to do so. Apply all the rituals on the Vocal Awareness Checklist. Allow the pitch to descend slightly as you sustain the tone. The sound should be completed by the time you're standing or sitting fully erect. Remember to keep your body relaxed and your breath and abdominal support intact while rising.

Notice how your body now stands straighter and taller in a more comfortable alignment with your hips. Everything falls more naturally into place. Be conscious of changes in your internal energy. Doing the Hanging Yawn-Sigh can give you an entirely new awareness of the production of sound throughout your body.

Optional: Record your impressions in your Vocal Power journal.

Alternate Warm-Up 3: Supported Yawn-Sigh

Upon occasion, you may substitute this exercise for the Hanging Yawn-Sigh. In this exercise, you will do the Yawn-Sigh while leaning forward against a supporting countertop or the back of a sofa. This technique enables you to get in touch with the powerful

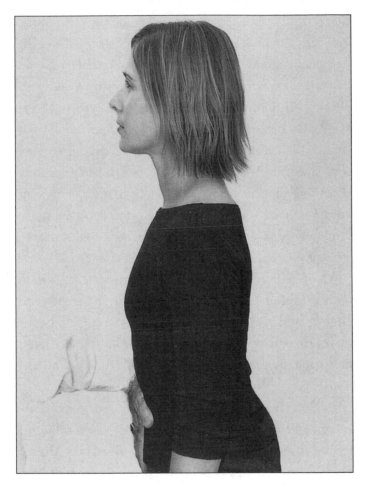

flow of breath and energy that soars through the nasal edge and arc like a geyser of water. It also introduces an emotional issue: trust of Self.

While maintaining your stature, begin by leaning forward and placing your abdomen against a stable supporting surface, a place where you do not fear falling. You may put a soft pillow between your stomach and the supporting surface for comfort. All your weight should be suspended. In this position, be sure to release your physical tension, taking extra care not to lock your feet.

Again, make a "V" with one hand and place it on your chin and jaw. Apply a gentle, downward pressure to ease your jaw open. Your mouth should be open to a width of about three fingers. Allow your tongue to rest against your bottom teeth. Keep your head level—you don't want it to drop forward as your jaw is released. Check your mirror to see that you're doing the technique correctly.

Now, do a Yawn-Sigh in this supported position on the sound of *Hah.* Allow the pitch to descend slightly and also to crescendo slightly (slowly increase in volume) as you sustain the tone. The sound should be extremely nasal. See the sound soar. Apply all the rituals on the Vocal Awareness Checklist.

I find this exercise very liberating. Since my body interprets that a bit of risk is involved—even though I know I am safely supported—it demands that I confront my feelings of being nervous and tense. If I am supported, why am I afraid of falling? What would I gain by overcoming this seemingly insurmountable act? There is freedom on the other side of any sort of anxiety that gets in the way of surrendering to the experience.

Optional: Record your impressions in your Vocal

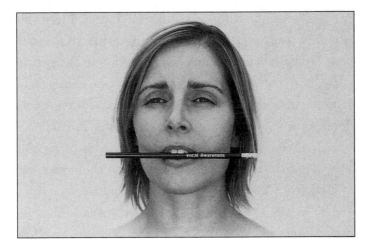

Power journal. This is a good opportunity to consider the issues of trust and support in your life and what—if anything—may be holding you back from giving and receiving them. Later, I'll talk more about the synergy between life and the vocal workout.

WARM-UP 4:
The Pencil Technique

In this exercise, you will be holding a pencil gently between your teeth as you do the Yawn-Sigh. Your vocal muscles will grow very quickly using the Pencil Technique, opening up a whole new range of Self-expression. But don't bite down! Please don't try it until you feel confident that you won't tense up while performing this technique.

Begin by standing or sitting in stature. Place the pencil in your mouth, gently holding it just in front of your eyeteeth. There is no need to hold onto the pencil with your hands. Allow your tongue to gently rest against your bottom teeth. Keep your head level—you don't want it to drop forward. Check your mirror.

First, take a moment to check for tension along the side of your jaw and in the soft spot on the underside of your chin. Release any tension you notice.

Now, do a Yawn-Sigh, with the pencil in your mouth, on the sound of *Hah.* You should focus on projecting this sound extremely nasally "over the top" of the pencil (not *under* it or *into* it) and very "forward" in your mouth (i.e., the front of your hard palate). It is important to "direct" the sound of your voice very specifically. Your pitch here isn't important. Simply keep your voice supported and focused. Apply all the rituals on the Vocal Awareness Checklist.

If done correctly, the sensation is that the sound is placed very far "forward" in your mouth.

Optional: Record your impressions in your Vocal Power journal.

The Second Aspect: The Bridge

Do you remember the analogy I made in Chapter 1 about driving lessons? You are now learning how to be a Formula One quality driver, not just a driver who drives competently on the highway. You already know how to speak, hold down a job, and manage the other basics of your life. Now you have chosen to train so that you will have a quality Voice and enjoy a higher quality life. The Bridge is a powerful technique that not only will enhance your Voice but will also boost your confidence and help you become more technically proficient.

On one level, the Bridge is a rehearsal process. You can apply this phase of the vocal workout to any text, song, or other "performance" material you're going to use—even words you're planning to say to your boss, your spouse, or your date. Your performance will become more fluid when you break the material down into more manageable pieces and apply the Vocal Awareness techniques to it. You can consciously embed the commands you choose into your muscular memory. As a result of this process, your body will learn to "think" before your mind does. Thus, you'll have the confidence of preparation.

Vocal Power can be rehearsed as long as is necessary until you have created the comfort you need to be your very best and feel most natural and free in the moment for which you are preparing. Performing artists of all types use similar methods to learn to inhabit their dance steps, arias, and soliloquies fully. Why shouldn't you benefit, too?

On another and deeper level, you are learning to become a master craftsman like legendary performers and athletes. These people are transcendent and rare; however, they are good models for the rest of us. Meryl Streep, Tiger Woods, Jussi Björling, Wynton Marsalis, Savion Glover, and Mikhail Baryshnikov hold themselves to the highest standards—and so should you. It is through your attention to detail within the training process that you will develop your technical ability to create aesthetically pleasing vocal tones. Once you gain this ability, you can deliberately tap into it every moment.

In later chapters, it will become crystal clear that the Vocal Awareness techniques as a whole system are the bridge to other parts of your life. That's why I keep reminding you that we should work on the Voice as a metaphor for the Self.

ACTIVITY:
The Bridge

In this integration exercise, you will be reciting text at the same time as you do one or more variations of the Yawn-Sigh. Once you understand the technique, it will be up to you to determine on a given day whether you prefer or need to do one variation, two variations, or all three. For the purpose of teaching, I will illustrate the Bridge successively using the Tongue Pull, the Two-

Finger Yawn-Sigh, and the Pencil Technique. Apply it
to the following text as you are learning:

♪ *When I speak, I need to be aware of projecting
my voice in a very specific arc.*

♪ *It doesn't matter whether it's loud or whether it's soft.*

♪ *The energy remains constant even though
the volume may change.*

Before you begin, please note: Your mouth and
tongue should be flaccid. The words and phrasing here
must be extremely fluid. Articulation is of no concern.
We are seeking freedom in the mouth. As a result, the
abdominals will provide better support, the jaw and
tongue will be less constricted, and the release of
energy will be greater.

First, position yourself for the Tongue Pull (see p.
106, if necessary). Stand or sit in stature. Place the
Vocal Awareness Checklist where you can easily read
it. Apply the rituals, breathing silently, deeply, and
lovingly down through your body.

Now, read the first line of text aloud—while lightly
pulling your tongue down—vocalizing it in the same
manner that you made the sound *Hah* in the Warm-Up
exercises. Speak very, very slowly, and very nasally elongating the phrases by extending the vowel sounds. (You
may even say the words one at a time if that helps you

maintain complete awareness.) Your subconscious mind responds to visual suggestion. Envisioning the "H" in particular makes vowels more open and connected and helps create more melody in the voice. Your spoken words should sound like the following text looks:

Whehn ah-ee speehk, ah-ee neehd to beeh
a-wehr av proh-jehc-ting ma-hee voh-ihce ihn
ah veh-ree speh-cih-fick aahrk.

As you apply Vocal Awareness in this way, don't leave pieces of the System out. Stand or sit in stature. Support the sound, don't rush, don't tighten your neck and shoulders, and keep it "musical," or aesthetically pleasing. Let it go high and low, but always maintain the same focus—the same nasal edge and arc. Focus on keeping your voice flowing and your tongue soft. Don't worry about articulation right now. Use as little mouth and tongue movement—without tension—as possible.

Now, position yourself for the Two-Finger Yawn-Sigh (see p. 109, if necessary). Stand or sit in stature. Apply the empowerment rituals. Inhale deeply and lovingly.

Then, read the second line of text aloud, elongating the vowels and speaking very slowly and nasally, as follows:

Iht dahz-nt mah-ter wheh-ther ihtz louhd
or wheh-ther ihtz saawhft.

Now, position yourself for the Pencil Technique (see p. 117, if necessary). Stand or sit in stature. Apply the empowerment rituals. Breathe for six to eight counts.

Then, read the third line of text, projecting your voice nasally "over" the top of the pencil, as follows:

> *Thah eh-ner-gee ihz cah-nstahnt ee-vehn*
> *thoh thah voh-lume meh-ee cheng.*

How did it feel? Listen to your audiotape. Do you notice additional richness, resonance, focus, and energy? Optional: Record your observations in your Vocal Power journal. When you feel comfortable with

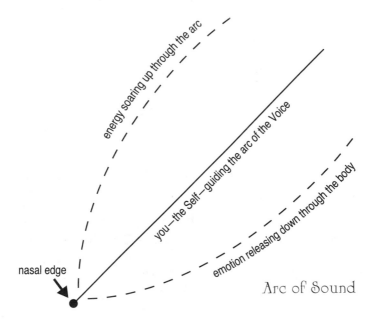

nasal edge

Arc of Sound

this exercise and can do it well, it will become one of your most valuable tools for immediately organizing your Voice in the way you intend.

Keep visualizing and focusing on the Nasal Edge and Arc of Sound.

Feel free to substitute any other text for the passage above. At the end of the book, you'll find some suggestions. It works equally as well with poetry or speeches, and for common phrases you might find yourself using in social situations, such as "Hi, my name is . . . It's nice to meet you." Anything, even the most seemingly mundane act of communication, can be made in Vocal Power. In Chapter 8 "Using Vocal Power for Singing," I'll explain how to practice the Bridge with songs.

The Third Aspect:
The Performance

You've finally arrived. It's time for you to put everything you've learned together. In this aspect of the Work, speak the same sentences you've just been working on in the Bridge freely without attempting to use any Yawn-Sigh techniques.

Begin by standing or sitting in stature. Check your mirror. Visualize the Vocal Awareness Checklist, then say:

When I speak, I need to be aware of projecting
my voice in a very specific arc. It doesn't matter

whether it's loud or whether it's soft. The energy
remains constant even though the volume may change.

Optional: Record your impressions in your Vocal
Power journal.

Congratulations! You have just learned the
complete vocal workout. Let's talk next about
designing a daily practice to support your developing
Vocal Power.

DESIGNING YOUR DAILY PRACTICE
Seven Minutes for Seven Days

Discover the value of the Vocal Awareness
method for yourself by practicing seven minutes a
day for the next seven days. If you do the vocal
workout faithfully during this week, you'll begin to
notice improvements in Vocal Power, and therefore
in your life, after only a few days. In time—as your
awareness grows—you can begin to develop your
own customized Vocal Awareness workout. (I'll give
you some suggestions.) But it's important that you
first have this direct experience of the benefits. Don't
take my word on it—do it!

In the box below, I have provided you with a
sample seven-minute workout routine. It's not necessary

that you spend the seven minutes of your practice session doing *exactly* these steps. However, it is important that your session include all three aspects of the vocal workout: the Warm-Up, the Bridge, and the Performance, and that you use all seven of the empowerment rituals on the Vocal Awareness Checklist. These are the nonnegotiable elements of the System that will enable you to make progress. Otherwise, your seven-minute routine should be determined by your individual needs. Spend an appropriate amount of time on each technique to perform it properly.

A Seven-Minute Workout

While standing in stature (remember the *invisible thread*), do the following:

First Aspect:

Minute 1: The Tongue Pull Yawn-Sigh,
Minute 2: The Two-Finger Yawn-Sigh,
Minute 3: The Pencil Technique Yawn-Sigh.

Second Aspect:

Minute 4: The Tongue Pull Yawn-Sigh with
text or song,

Minute 5: The Two-Finger Yawn-Sigh with
   text or song,
Minute 6: The Pencil Technique Yawn-Sigh
   with text or song.

Third Aspect:

Minute 7: The Performance.

Please feel free to expand the duration of your workout session if you have the time and feel ready to make the commitment. Seven minutes is the minimum guideline. Experience has taught me that people respond best to direct experiences. Your success will be found through doing it. Since this system is an integration of mind/body/spirit, you won't gain confidence and see results by merely reading or thinking about it. In other words, give yourself the gift of the experience without passing judgment ahead of time. This is a good way to take a strong and steady first step on your new path to Vocal Power.

Customizing Your Daily Routine

Believe it or not, you are in a better position to know your vocal challenges than anyone else. So even though the exercises in the vocal workout have a specific structure that you must apply diligently, your daily workout routine has a certain amount of flexibility. There are also variations on the exercises that you can try as your technical abilities become stronger.

Please be aware that although your practice sessions should be a regular part of your day, your exercises should never become *routine*. You are breaking longstanding, *unconscious* vocal habits. Don't replace them with new ones. Stay focused and alert.

At the beginning of a session, set a specific intention about what you're going to work on, such as any one of the empowerment rituals (e.g., *See the Nasal Edge and Arc of Sound* or *Take My Time*). Use this intention to anchor your mental focus initially. Then, as you proceed, follow the natural progression that develops and let your discoveries lead your focus. Every session will be unique in subtle or obvious ways.

Experiment with different qualities of sound making in your daily sessions:

- ♪ Loud/soft,
- ♪ High/low,
- ♪ Duration,
- ♪ Emotion,
- ♪ Vowels.

This last suggestion may prove especially interesting. Once you have grown confident using the *Hah* sound (as in "hat") to perform the exercises, you may substitute other vowel sounds. Always begin with the *Hah*, which is your initial mental anchor, and blend another vowel out of it. Play with the sounds of:

♪ *Ha* (as in "ha ha ha"): This should sound like an elongated *Hah ah* [with a conscious *plié* connecting them].

♪ *He* (as in "heat"): This should sound like an elongated *Hah eeh* [with a conscious *plié* connecting them].

♪ *Hoo* (as in "hoot"): This should sound like an elongated *Hah ooh* [with a conscious *plié* connecting them].

Also try selecting different texts to work on in different sessions. Choose those that inspire and move you in some way. Poetry can be a wonderful adjunct to the Work. Some suggestions are listed in the back of the book.

♪ Sovereignty means "supreme excellence, or an example of it."

The Vocal Power Journey

The Vocal Awareness method and the Vocal Power journey is a process of developing conscious awareness. Your goal is sovereignty—complete personal empowerment. You cannot make either a big change or a simple adjustment until you can recognize exactly what's not working (or is working) and how to find a solution. Can you see that this is more than one step in a process? Awareness must always come first. Implementing a solution comes later. The process you're now learning is how to:

- ♪ Observe/Notice,
- ♪ Analyze/Dialogue,
- ♪ Solve/Experiment,
- ♪ Integrate/Implement.

Analysis takes place through an internal dialogue in which you use your observations, notes, and any other sources of feedback to stimulate the development of your Self-awareness. It's an ongoing conversation in which you learn to ask the questions that will lead you to do better than you already are and help you recognize when you're doing just fine. This is the way you can begin to command your mental focus and establish a visceral connection with your words and how they sound and feel. Frankly, it's something most of us were never taught to do.

One of my students is a highly successful professional who has worked with the Vocal Awareness method on a daily basis for the past three years with great integrity and dedication. In his sessions, he works on songs and speeches he's going to deliver, and prepares for business encounters. After this time, he continues to make discoveries. His ability to discern how he is communicating and to make choices about the way he will be perceived has progressed through his daily application of the techniques. There are always more levels to realize.

Another student is a financial analyst who has enhanced his creativity and become less circumspect and judgmental. He has changed his entire style of business since he began the Work and this journey has helped him solicit new clients and become more successful.

Here is an imaginary dialogue you might have as you are practicing the Tongue Pull. (Remember to have your Checklist while practicing and to observe yourself in a mirror while taping your exercise.) Let's say that you've just completed one and noticed that it seemed rushed and you didn't particularly like the quality of the sound. You might go through this sequence:

1. Did I remember to surrender and *Allow a Silent, Loving, Down-through-my-body Breath*

before I began? Let me try it again to see if that helps. (You do it again.)

2. Okay. That helped me *Take My Time* and I felt more aware. The sound of the quality is better but is still not enough. My tongue seems a bit tense. This time I'm going to place my focus on *Loving and Letting Go*. (You do it again.)

3. That felt better. I enjoyed it more. But what's up with the tone? It could be more pleasing and resonant. Okay, I'm feeling annoyed now. There's that old emotional issue about being "perfect." Remember, I can take all the time I need—this isn't a race and I don't need to impress anyone. I'm going to allow a moment and breathe— lovingly—until this passes. (You do.) Okay, this time I'll keep what I already learned but focus more on my Nasal Edge and Arc of Sound. (You do the exercise again.)

4. Something positive seems to be happening, but I'm not sure what. Let me visualize sending my energy more effectively up through the arc. (You do another one right away.)

5. Yes! That was what I needed. I felt my Voice soaring and my abdominal support was

stronger. It sounded good. Yay! I'm going to do it again just for fun. (You do. Then you record your impressions in your notebook.)

The Importance of Feedback

I recently taught a Vocal Awareness workshop in an adult learning center wherein I had several participants stand at the front of the class to perform different exercises. I often use this method not only to illustrate the various elements of the vocal workout and the kinds of adjustments that need to be made but also so that my students can get on the spot feedback from their peers. As you'll soon find out, it is not always easy to be objective about your own voice or the subtle shifts in quality that can result from making different adjustments. Usually, they find the opportunity to give and receive honest feedback enormously helpful. In addition, this method illustrates that everyone shares more or less the same issues and challenges. Before you can pinpoint them in your own behavior, however, it's often easier to see them demonstrated by another person.

On this particular occasion, I had the participants say only one or two sentences about their careers. A woman in her late-20s told the group: "I work in audio-visual communications. I write and edit content for an online newsletter." I had her sit in stature, inhale more lovingly before speaking, and stop twitching her leg beneath the table. It only took a few moments. When she repeated her statement, the class reported that her voice already sounded "stronger and less breathy" although I hadn't even worked on her "voice." A middle-aged gentleman then told me: "I am involved with investments. I manage my personal portfolio." Again, the improvement was immediate once he sat up, put both of his feet firmly on the floor, and *committed* to what he was saying. He had complained that his voice sounded too nasal, whereas I recognized his voice as lacking energy and dynamism. It only seemed nasal because the way he used his voice was technically inefficient. The class could hear a difference after just those few simple adjustments even though he could not. He needed their feedback.

When you practice the vocal workout at home, your two best friends are going to be your mirror and your tape recorder or video camera. You cannot progress without them. Consider this: Could you learn to be a wonderful dancer without looking in a mirror? Probably not—if you truly wanted to dance well. Likewise, you cannot do this work well without a mirror because most people do not have much kines-thetic awareness, meaning a sense of how their bodies move. For example, you might not even know where your tongue is located. Without even knowing it, you may pull your tongue backward when your mouth opens instead of allowing it to lay forward gently. But in a mirror, you can see this as it occurs and then correct it. Similarly, the tape recorder or video camera is going to enable you to hear and see the kinds of things that my workshop participants reported to each other. It will help you notice your subtle improvements.

All mastery is achieved only when we master the subtleties of a form. Profound discoveries are made in the mastery of these subtle distinctions.

Success Tip:
Record Your Observations and Impressions

As you will soon discover, practicing the Vocal Awareness method is a meticulous process of outward and inward development, similar in certain respects to a science experiment. As a researcher, you are in unknown territory and need to collect data on the impact of these techniques. It is also like a detective story wherein you are seeking clues. As an investigator, you are piecing together the mystery of your identity: your foibles, fears, ecstasies, dreams, and motivations.

You have the option of keeping a journal that is devoted exclusively to your practice sessions and "performances." This will provide you with a means to track your progress and reflect on every level of the experience. Consider recording impressions about your:

♪ Body,

♪ Sound,

♪ Thoughts,

♪ Emotions,

♪ Attitudes,

♪ Energy.

Remember: This journal doesn't have to be an elaborate record. You will simply jot down a few notes on your sessions and any discoveries you make. In each new day's practice, you then refer to your notes and incorporate what you have already learned. Question and observe, as these speed the learning process.

Success Tip:
Game Film

Professional athletes have developed extraordinary training methods and protocols. One of these is the concept of "game film." They videotape every game they play or race they run or bike in order to review it, analyze it, and use what they learn the next time. They know that actual performances put them under greater pressure than practice sessions. In these spontaneous and demanding circumstances, they either rise to the occasion or don't. But their dedication to being the best means they want to understand the nuances of both success and failure so they can thoroughly improve.

The use of "game film" is not limited to athletes. One time I went with friends to hear Mel Torme sing at a sweet little jazz club on the Upper East Side of Manhattan. After the gig, Mel came over and sat with us, and I observed that he had a stack of audiotapes with him. It turned out they were recordings of the show. Even though at that time he'd already been in show business for 52 years, he still taped every performance so he could review his work. That's "game film," too.

In developing Vocal Power, you can use "game film" by sticking a small tape recorder in your pocket when you go on job interviews or have conversations with your colleagues. If you feel any ethical qualms, make a point of asking for permission first. Record your own side of telephone conversations and play them back later. Have someone shoot a videotape when you're giving a lecture, presentation, or performing in any other way. You'll be amazed at how much you'll discover about your Voice.

"Game film" is one of the tools that will enable you to be a better Self-coach.

TAKING THE NEXT STEP

As you continue your Vocal Power journey, you will learn to discover what I call the *hub* of the Voice—the core of who you truly are. Just as spokes extend from the central hub of a bicycle wheel, there are various "spokes" that come from the hub of your Voice. These represent your multiple sub-personalities metaphorically: the warrior, the victim, the parent, the child, the teacher, the lover, and so forth. But they aren't necessarily coming out of a congruent Voice yet—a balanced and integrated Voice that is open and fluid, emerging *consciously* from that hub. Once you discover the hub of your Voice, you'll begin to learn how to tap into it *always* and express the myriad of possibilities that exist within you. You'll learn how to express them consistently from the same congruent, balanced core.

You'll find numerous examples in later chapters of using daily practice sessions to improve your posture, overcome fear and other emotional blocks, develop confidence and Self-esteem, and enhance your career and social life. In the next chapter, we're going to talk about the health benefits of Vocal Power.

5 Health Benefits of Vocal Power

Sound is a nutrient for our
Spirit as well as our body.
—Robert Gass

You have already learned the basics of the vocal workout. The length of time it will take you to master these Vocal Awareness techniques depends on what you bring to your practice: the extent of your dedication, how deeply rooted your habits are, and also how badly you want it. By performing the vocal workout regularly, you'll soon become more aware of your vocal health or lack of health. You will begin to notice everything that supports your Voice and encourages it to blossom, as well as everything that impedes your Voice, especially the production of sound. This chapter focuses on what these health problems may be and describe how, as a result of your vocal workouts, some will gradually abate of their own accord. Another aspect of your journey to Vocal Power will also be covered here: the importance of learning proper "vocal hygiene" or how to tend to your voice.

IMPROVING HEALTH
What Is Ailing Us?

As infants, we make sounds to explore our personal universe. We not only make sounds to express what we want but also babble "goo goo" and "ga ga" simply to express our sense of aliveness—to be our Selves. But we also learn early on to silence our Voices. In childhood, our parents often hush us so that we will be quiet and nondisruptive in our surroundings. Sitting on mommy or daddy's lap in a church, mosque, temple, or synagogue, for instance, we might receive a gentle pat on the back and a "Shhh." To be accepted and maintain their love, we shut down our organic—unrestricted—Voice over time. Or in an angry home, where disapproval is frightening, we learn to be silent in order to avoid the possibility of being hurt. By the time we are adults, we regularly encounter social situations that do not allow for the free expression of our feelings. The resulting confusion and frustration create tension in our tongue and jaw, stifle the flow of air, and set up other blocks that hinder our ability to make sound. These conditions also contribute to many stress-related health problems, such as headaches, back pain, indigestion, hypertension, and insomnia.

The most efficient way to channel our emotional and physical energy—in life and in communication—

is through the breath. This airflow communicates what's inside us to the outside world. We abuse our voices when we are unable to support sound making with an intense and focused flow of breath and abdominal support. Thus, when we scream or shout in joy and anger, we often end up hoarse. But have you ever heard a hoarse infant? No. Infants can scream or cry indefinitely because, in part, they are still using a primal breathing pattern. When you watch infants breathe, air flows down through their bodies; their abdomens naturally rise. When they cry, their abdominal muscles pull upward and inward and support the sound instinctively—perfectly.

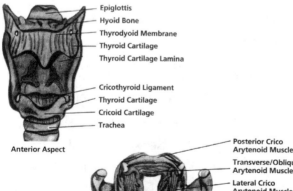

Epiglottis
Hyoid Bone
Thyrodyoid Membrane
Thyroid Cartilage
Thyroid Cartilage Lamina

Cricothyroid Ligament
Thyroid Cartilage
Cricoid Cartilage
Trachea

Anterior Aspect

Posterior Crico
Arytenoid Muscle
Transverse/Oblique
Arytenoid Muscles
Lateral Crico
Arytenoid Muscle
Crycothyroid Muscle
Thyro-Arytenoid Muscle
Vocalis Muscle
Vocal Ligament
Thyroid Cartilage

**Intrinsic Muscles
of the Larynx**

As adults, we must relearn the natural, intrinsic way of breathing and sound making that we gave away as we grew up if we want to experience excellent health and speak or sing better. The vocal passage bears the brunt of holding back our passion, joy, confusion, and pain. The vocal folds go into spasm and the ligaments and membranes surrounding the larynx constrict. All the other muscles in our bodies contract in sympathy. When we are under sustained emotional stress, we tend to build up patterns of muscular tension throughout our bodies. However, by doing the Vocal Awareness techniques, you will start to reclaim your natural ability to breathe and freely express yourself. You'll get back in touch with the hub of your Voice.

Among the myriad of health benefits that result from this process, you will:

♪ Reduce tension in your jaw, tongue, neck, and shoulders, and other areas of the body where emotional stress typically is held;

♪ Look better, because your endorphin levels will rise and you'll be getting more oxygen, as well as reducing facial tension;

♪ Feel energized, for the same reasons as above;

♪ Feel energized because, instead of wasting energy on Self-restraint, you'll learn to move positively to advance your life and live more fully;

♪ Boost your immunity, because endorphins and proper breathing are relaxing and healthful in so many respects; and,

♪ Elevate your spirits, for it will be as though a burden has been lifted, as you take better care of your Self and feel better in the ways I have described.

Reducing Jaw Tension

One of the most common places to hold tension is in the muscles of the jaw. Incredibly, the jaw is capable of producing between 6,000 and 10,000 pounds of pressure per square inch. So as you can imagine, frequent jaw clenching or grinding of the teeth puts the whole structure of the jaw—its muscles, bones, and soft tissues—under considerable stress. With 56 moving parts, the temporomandibular joints beside your ears are the most complex joints in the body. They are sensitive and can become painful, swollen, and fail to function correctly. This group of symptoms is collectively referred to as temporomandibular joint syndrome ("TMJ").

Releasing jaw tension is vital to good vocal production. You can begin to do so by massaging the joint area with your fingers as often as possible, as well as the muscles along the sides of your lower jaw. Gently massage the soft tissue area for three to four minutes at night before you go to sleep and in the morning upon awakening. The action is similar to kneading dough when you're baking bread. Perform some deep pressure massages, pushing into tender spots—but never press to the point of pain, only to create relief. Make ten circles in one direction, then reverse direction and make another ten circles. The Jaw Release technique will also help you (see p. 67, if necessary).

It can be very useful to set a clear intention at bedtime not to clench your teeth during the night. Your subconscious mind does respond to direct suggestions. If possible, go to sleep listening to soft music, classical music, or a relaxation tape. Do all these steps consistently for a couple of weeks along with the vocal workout, and your TMJ problems will begin to cease. The most severe case I have seen only took a month to cure. The TMJ may flare up again in a moment of stress, but now you possess the means to get rid of it.

Reducing Tongue Tension

Curiously, the tongue is the strongest muscle per diameter in the body. As you can see in the illustration below, two very thick and powerful muscles, called the "genioglossus" and "geniohyoid," form its base. All parts of the tongue can hold a lot of tension.

Stop reading for a moment and look in the mirror. Open your mouth nice and wide, and notice what your tongue does. Most likely, it pulls back and covers your throat. At a subconscious level, this action is an attempt to "protect" us from exposure. Unfortunately, as the tongue tenses and pulls back, it inhibits our freedom of expression. It psychologically locks us up and suffocates us. It also constricts sound so that it is less colorful and expressive in tone, harsher, and more brittle.

As you become more emotionally and technically secure in communicating, this problem will resolve. In the meantime, the Tongue Pull in the vocal workout is an excellent means of reducing tongue tension. It is

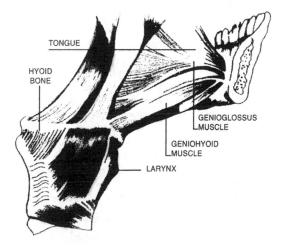

also a good idea to remind yourself at different points throughout the day to allow your tongue to release and lay forward gently, whenever practical, resting against the back of your bottom teeth.

Raising Your Endorphin Levels

Did you ever wonder why you feel so good after a deep belly laugh? Or why aerobic exercise gives you a "runner's high"? The reason for both is the presence of endorphins in your bloodstream. Endorphins are naturally forming brain chemicals that have pain-relieving properties similar to morphine. Besides behaving as regulators of pain and stress, endorphins also produce feelings of euphoria, improve the circulation of the blood, help enhance memory, and increase immunity. Pretty amazing, aren't they?

The good news is that the Vocal Awareness techniques will raise your endorphin levels, since deep breathing and singing stimulate your body to release them. As a result, you will look better. You will have a smile more frequently on your face, your eyes will be brighter, your cheeks rosier, and your facial tension will dissipate. In addition, you'll feel better. You're going to gain mental clarity and a more positive outlook on life. So if you're ever strapped for time or need a quick boost, just remember that doing even a single brief Vocal Awareness technique can literally and instantaneously enhance your Voice.

BASIC VOCAL HYGIENE

What can you do when you have a cold, travel by airplane, or feel fatigued? Some health problems, such as a dry or sore throat, a dry mouth, hoarseness, and excess saliva, can be handled expeditiously. But even psychomotor difficulties, such as stuttering and lisping, can begin to be dealt with by using simple and straightforward measures. Let's take a look at some ways to help keep your voice in working order.

Drink Plenty of Fluids

Everyone needs to drink plenty of fluids. I recommend that you consume at least eight to 12 glasses of water each day at room temperature—not too hot and not too cold. Extreme temperatures affect the vocal folds and surrounding areas and do not allow them to stay neutral. As an illustration, consider how placing a hot compress on a wound causes the blood vessels in that area to expand. Conversely, placing a cold compress constricts the blood vessels. Well, the same thing happens to the blood vessels and mucous membranes inside your throat. Neutral is preferable. During your vocal workouts, keep a glass or bottle of water handy and sip from it frequently.

In addition to water, you may enjoy drinking honey and lemon in warm water, or warm tea—just not too hot! I often squeeze the juice of one-quarter lemon into my water glass. Coffee tends to dry out the mucous membranes and therefore should be limited.

Warm-Up

If you were a professional athlete or dancer, you would always stretch your body before competing or performing for at least 30 to 45 minutes. Now, everyday when you go out into the world using your voice to represent who you are, you must think of yourself as a *professional voice user*. Thus, it is not unreasonable to ask you to do a warm-up. This does not have to be a big deal; a few minutes can suffice. For this purpose, use the daily vocal workout you learned in Chapter 4. Among other things, you are warming up your larynx, which is both the smallest and most complex muscle in the body. And interestingly, it is the only muscle that functions solely through the movement of air.

When You Have a Cold, Sore Throat, or Hoarseness

If you are feeling poorly and this condition involves your throat, use your voice as little as possible. Put yourself on at least 12 to 24 hours of complete vocal rest, if possible, locking yourself away in the proverbial closet. However, if vocal rest is unrealistic to expect, do not make the mistake of thinking you are saving your voice by whispering—you are actually working it harder! Whispering is performed in part by a tiny muscle called the crycothyroid that connects to the lower rear part of the larynx. This is not the strongest part of the vocal mechanism, and therefore, it tires and wears out a lot faster.

Do your warm-up exercises *very* gently, *very* nasally, *very* slowly, and *very* accurately—and only for a few minutes, without any dramatics. Use moderate dynamics: not too loud or too soft. Be very specific, making sure that as you are doing the vocal work you are integrating the mind/body/spirit connection. Double-check yourself to ensure that you are really slowing down rather than tensing up. This gentle approach is necessary because our bodies compensate when we don't feel well. Then we tend to speak more frugally with worse posture: the head dips, the shoulders tighten, and the breath shortens. This happens unconsciously.

Use the rituals *Pay Attention/Deeper Listening* and *Take My Time*. When you do not feel well vocally and/or physically, the most important thing you can do is breathe. Try to allow your six- to eight-count silent inhalations to be done even more mindfully and lovingly than usual. Slow down your speech so that you have more time to engage the conscious mind to coordinate it. Do not speak too loudly; maintain moderate dynamics.

During the vocal workout, you are training your mind's eye to *See the Nasal Edge and Arc of Sound*, and this will now support your voice. It can be extremely helpful to visualize your arc of sound—not your pitch—lifting a little bit higher than it usually does. As you speak, locate the *internal lift*, a sense that your soft palate is lifting way up inside but with no forcing or added tension. Some people refer to this feeling as an "inner smile" within the mouth. (To create this, I don't want you to spread your mouth wide in a "grin," however, or to fixate on the back of your throat.) It can take some time to become attuned to this sensation, but after a while it will begin to happen on its own and sustain itself.

Lucie Arnaz is a wonderful singer, dancer, and actress and has been a student of mine for over 20 years. Several years ago, she was performing at Rainbow and Stars, a once great nightclub at the top of Rockefeller Center in New York City, which has since closed. She thought she was doing a good thing for herself by taking bee pollen. Unfortunately, she had an allergic reaction. Both her vocal tract and her larynx became so inflamed that she could not vocalize prior to the show. If you had heard her speak right then, you would never have thought she would be able to sing at all that evening, let alone give a masterful performance. However, Lucie had already been working with the Vocal Awareness method for many years, and it was fully integrated into her.

I gave her the same advice I wrote above. "You *really* have to *See the Nasal Edge and Arc of Sound* and to remain aware of your breathing. Keep your neck and shoulders released, and use every other tool on the Vocal Awareness Checklist." Because Lucie had studied and practiced so diligently over the years, she was able to draw upon her mind/body/spirit integration masterfully. Although her throat was raw and inflamed, she went on stage and gave one of the finest performances of her career. She did not enjoy it as much as usual because she had to concentrate more. However, she did not "miss a trick." Lucie didn't cut any numbers, she didn't modify any of her high notes, and she didn't do anything less than give the best of her Self possible. In a word, she was "extraordinary." This is an example of how using the techniques effectively really works.

Excess Mucous

One of the worst things you can do to your larynx is to clear your throat. Clearing the throat badly irritates the vocal mechanism, wearing it down much like grinding gears in a car. To function efficiently, the vocal folds need air. Throat clearing causes the vocal folds to rub together without air—like grinding the gears in a car with a stick shift—and therefore hurts the voice. Instead, allow saliva to build up in your mouth and then swallow. Or cough gently to loosen mucous on the vocal folds and swallow. This should be a rather breathy cough, not percussive or hacking. The gentle approach will probably clear the vocal folds and give you the relief you are seeking.

Sucking on lozenges can also be helpful. I recommend Grether's blackcurrant or redcurrant pastilles, an over-the-counter brand of lozenges made in Switzerland from an old English recipe. These are available in many drugstores and markets. They contain glycerin, which is extremely soothing to the vocal folds. Old-fashioned Smith Brothers cherry lozenges are also fine. But stay away from menthol-coated drops, as they can sometimes irritate the throat.

Gargling can sometimes contribute to cleaning out mucous, even though it doesn't clean very far down the throat. A simple recipe is to mix one tablespoon of apple cider vinegar into six ounces of warm water. That's enough for two or three shots of gargle. Take a mouthful, gargle it in the back of your throat, and then expel it. Please note: I advise you *not* to make noise as you gargle—silent gargling is more healthful.

Sugar creates mucous and thus should be avoided. So be aware that drinking regular soda is not a good way to get your daily liquids. Popular brands, such as Coca-Cola, contain about one teaspoon of sugar per ounce. So there are 12 teaspoons of sugar in an average bottle or can! This high syrup content can be as harmful to the vocal folds as the extreme cold temperatures at which people tend to drink their sodas.

Alcoholic beverages can sometimes produce excess mucous as well. Beverages such as red wine usually contain tannins, which are added during production. If you need your voice to be at its best for a presentation or performance, it is therefore wise not to drink red wine immediately beforehand. White wine does not have the same adverse effect. But grain alcohol, vodka, and beer can cause a histaminic, or allergic reaction, and also can create mucous.

Dairy products are notorious for producing mucous. When your voice needs to be optimal or at a performance level, eliminate or minimize your consumption of milk and cream.

Remember that these new ways of clearing your throat may not seem as emotionally satisfying, but they actually work. Doing it the other way actually doesn't!

When You're Tired

When the body is fatigued, the voice is generally the first outward sign of it. Vocal exhaustion is heard immediately and gets expressed in breathiness, hoarseness, and a lack of support and energy. So, if this is your condition, it is important to understand that being tired makes you susceptible to vocal injury. Now more than ever, you must be acutely aware of using good vocal technique. Apply the principles of Vocal Awareness that you learned in Chapters 3 and 4. Better abdominal support, better breathing, and better attention to the Nasal Edge and Arc of Sound are required. Also, get some rest!

Airplane Travel

When I was in graduate school, my voice science classmates and I conducted an experiment that included taking a sound-level meter into the cabin of a jet. According to this device, the stress on the vocal folds when speaking inside the plane with the engines churning was the equivalent of shouting when standing by the afterburner of the jet. Thus, speaking over the noise level in airplanes clearly places a tremendous strain on the larynx. The next time you fly, notice how many hoarse flight attendants there are.

If you travel a great deal by airplane, as I do, and need to use your voice energetically for business as soon as you arrive at your destination, try to speak infrequently or not at all while on the plane. When you must speak while flying, do so as quietly as possible and diligently apply the Nasal Edge and Arc of Sound techniques you have learned. Also make sure to drink plenty of room temperature water in order to stay properly hydrated.

Women's Voices

If you are a woman, it's important to understand that your vocal folds are affected by your menstrual cycle. For instance, if swelling is a problem prior to or during menses, it will occur in the vocal folds, as well as elsewhere in your body. Furthermore, you are more susceptible to vocal strain during menstruation. Your voice is not as flexible then as it normally is due to the slight swelling throughout your body. So, if you must use your voice at a professional level for speaking or singing during your menses, it is vital to take more time than usual to warm up your voice.

Of course, some women are severely affected by menstruation, others only minimally. Therefore, your vocal needs at this time of the month will be individual. Try to become more aware of your needs.

Interestingly, if you were to examine samples of tissue from both the larynx and the cervix, you would not be able to tell one from another. These are the only two parts of the human anatomy that have identical tissue; you cannot distinguish one from the other from the color and mucosal counts.

Avoid Smoking

It should go without saying that smoking is an unhealthful habit for many reasons, but it is especially destructive to the professional voice user. The problem is not so much the smoke as the heat. Subjecting your vocal folds to 2,000 to 3,000 degree heat severely dries out the mucous membranes. As a result, the membranes then oversecrete mucous to protect themselves. While the mucous levels increase, new layers of tissue are formed on the vocal folds, which thicken, redden, and enlarge the muscles. As this happens, the throat has to be cleared more often, which irritates the vocal tract and the vocal folds even more.

Nodules and Granulomas

Nodules, often referred to as "nodes," are a common condition that occurs in the posterior, or upper third of the larynx, which produces the high part of your voice. Nodes can develop in as quickly as 24 hours or over a long period of time. They result either from stress or, more often, from using your voice improperly. More specifically, nodes develop by speaking too loudly, too fast, with too much tension, or without enough support—in other words, by failing to apply good vocal technique.

Granulomas are commonly known as "contact ulcers." They occur in the anterior third of the larynx, the area that produces the low part of your voice, when the larynx is forced against the hyoid bone (see p. 141 for illustration). Over time, an ulcer—or hole—forms in the vocal folds, thus severely limiting vocalization. This results from poor vocal technique, specifically trying to create a low voice improperly—or from extensive coughing or shouting—that pushes the speaking voice too low for its natural pitch range.

Both conditions must be treated by an otolaryngologist—an ear, nose, and throat doctor with specialized training—working in conjunction with a speech pathologist, a speech therapist, or a superior voice teacher. If caught early enough and treated thoughtfully with vocal therapy, they can be healed. In addition, you need good retraining in vocal technique; otherwise, the problems come back. If these conditions are not dealt with properly, surgery may become necessary.

If a doctor tells you that you have such a serious vocal condition, always get at least two, if not three, opinions before acting. Sometimes they can be mistaken. Several years ago, I was on the road with a voice student who had developed a habit of drinking heavily after his singing appearances. For some time I'd been advising him not to do this, since it could adversely affect his voice—even cause him to lose it. And finally, it happened on an evening when he was scheduled to do two sets of a nightclub act. During the first show he sang relatively well, although he noticed a little hoarseness. Then between shows, he lost his voice almost instantly and couldn't go out for the second show. Of course, he was in a panic so I helped him track down a laryngologist in the middle of the night. But he went to the doctor by himself. Later that night, he came back and told me that the doctor said he had nodules.

"You no more have nodules than I can jump off buildings and fly," I replied. "You are simply having a histaminic reaction to all the vodka you keep drinking."

Of course, his answer was, "But the doctor saw them."

"That doctor is crazy. If you have nodules, I swear to you that I will write you a check for all the money you've spent with me for lessons over the years." I was dead serious. And I could make this kind of wager because I knew his history. I also instinctively knew I was right.

In any event, at 1:00 A.M., I called and awakened the late, great, world famous otolaryngologist, Dr. Wilbur Gould, in New York City. Dr. Gould told me to bring my client to his office the next morning, which I did. Thirty seconds into the examination, he confirmed my advice. "You're having a histaminic reaction to the alcohol you pour down your throat. Quit drinking temporarily." Needless to say, my client was very relieved. Dr. Gould also prescribed some medication, and I put my client on a vocal therapy regimen. Shortly thereafter, he fully recovered and went back on stage.

Psychomotor Conditions

A gentleman named Klaus has been my student for over six years, and I have seen him go through a remarkable personal transformation. Now in his early 60s, he struggled for about 20 years with a condition known as "severe spasmodic dysphonia," in which you often cannot get closure on the vocal folds when you're breathing and speaking. Frequently, this triggers a panic response, making the problem even worse. As you can imagine, it is a serious challenge that is physically, emotionally, and socially debilitating. Doctors often try to ameliorate such spasms with remedies that include using plastic inserts or injecting the vocal tract with botox to paralyze it. In our sessions, we've been dealing with his spasmodic dysphonia through Vocal Awareness and singing. A year or two ago, Klaus retired from the bank where he worked for virtually his entire career. He has a truly beautiful tenor voice that got him accepted into a choir, and he has been happier ever since.

Three years ago, Klaus came to my workshop at the Esalen Institute. For his closing ceremony presentation, he first played a tape from his very first lesson with me and then he spoke to the audience impeccably. I had honestly forgotten what he sounded like at the time I met him, and the improvement was so profound and deeply moving that it made many of us cry. Not only has the progress he has made been rewarding for him—because he can *really* speak and sing now—but I am rewarded as well.

There is a number of vocal challenges that involve some malfunction of the physical mechanisms of speech and also have a psychological dimension. The most common of these are stuttering and lisping, although there are more severe conditions. People who experience one of these problems may find that it severely affects their sense of Self. It creates anxiety and frustration and gets in the way of an otherwise smooth flow of living life on their own terms. The Vocal Awareness method holds many keys to coping with psychomotor challenges effectively. However, since muscles are being exercised and strengthened, this has to be a regular lifelong commitment or the challenges will return.

Every time I'm given the opportunity to deal intimately with people who experience these types of vocal challenges, it reconfirms how valuable Vocal Awareness is in managing psychomotor conditions. I've observed that when Klaus is not in the *detail* of the Work, he'll rush his breath and won't speak or sing as well. Even the slightest rush throws off his voice. Granted sometimes he thinks he can cut corners, but he doesn't really have that option. He cannot rush— period. Luckily for Klaus, I'm stuck to him like a fly caught on flypaper, offering him constant reminders to stay conscious and be a meticulous artist—a conscientious communicator.

Stuttering and Lisping

Stuttering, like spasmodic dysphonia, usually has an emotional as well as a physiological cause. The great American actor, James Earl Jones, is a lifetime stutterer who has always been painfully shy. Responding to a query about his stuttering during an interview printed in the December 19, 1995 issue of the *Los Angeles Times*, Jones replied:

> My voice is a gift that often doesn't work. I still have difficulty getting thoughts out, so my goal is to say something with clarity. I left the church at the age of 14 because I couldn't do Sunday school recitations without the kids laughing . . . . But the great Olympic runner Wilma Rudolph had serious leg problems. [Dancer] Gwen Verdon had rickets as a child. Demosthenes put pebbles in his mouth and became a great orator. If you can acknowledge a weak muscle and exercise it, it can define your life.

Aware of his "weakness," Jones chose to conquer it. And if you share this problem, so can you. Stuttering can be managed, and even eradicated through maintaining conscious awareness, by integrating your mind/body/spirit, and by applying good vocal technique—all of which the Vocal Awareness method teaches you. Singing is another wonderful tool to counteract stuttering. It strengthens the vocal muscles, and creates better coordination and better-timed coordination. It also engages the voice in elongated vowel sounds rather than spasmodic bursts of sound. When singing, the vocal folds stay tautly stretched longer because the pressure flow of air is being sustained to hold out notes. In addition, as I mentioned near the beginning of the chapter, singing raises endorphin levels, so that singers feel healthier and happier, too.

Lisping is another condition that's helped by singing. Both are also aided by practicing the Vocal Awareness exercises that incorporate the Yawn-Sigh. If you lisp or stutter, you can also use the following activity to help address tongue and lip tension.

ACTIVITY:
Extending Your Voiced Consonants

This activity will benefit anyone who wants to articulate consonants better.

Begin by making a long *Zzzzz* sound. This vibrates the tip of the tongue with intensifying pressure. An intensified pressure flow of air requires good abdominal support. Therefore, the whole vocal mechanism functions more easily and effectively. Then, do the same exercise with other voiced consonants (V, D, B, G, and J). Extend them and experience their vibrations.

A voiced consonant is a sound that vibrates in the vocal tract—V versus F, D versus T, B versus P, and Z versus S. The unvoiced consonants in these pairs do not have the same vibratory intensity although the tongue placement is almost identical.

A Final Thought

As you become more conscious of your Voice by practicing your daily vocal workouts, you'll become more attuned to your health. Then, you can address problems that may arise in a timely manner. Awareness always precedes action. Please also keep in mind that many vocal health challenges can be avoided simply by applying good technique.

6
The Importance of
Body Language

Nor do not saw the air too much
with your hand thus, but use all gently . . .
—William Shakespeare

Have you ever caught yourself compulsively twirling a strand of hair around your finger? Do you ever jiggle your leg beneath the table? When you're introduced to somebody, is it hard for you to maintain eye contact? Are you a "hand-talker" who continually repeats the same gestures over and over again? (It's okay to use your hands but just not to be repetitive with these gestures.) Each one of these physical habits can detract from Vocal Power. For as you'll learn in this chapter, body language is an extremely important component of the image you project to the world.

It doesn't matter whether we are in an office meeting, on a date, or shopping at the local mall: Fifty-five percent of any spoken message we communicate comes through our body language. When body language is *consciously* aligned with a chosen persona, our presence will be perceived as authentic, commanding, and relaxed. But body language may include information we do not intend, or would prefer not to communicate, such as "I'm nervous," or "I'm unavailable to you." It can even give others a false impression about us, as it did in the following case of one of my students.

When I met this highly motivated businessman, who happens to be six feet five inches tall, his original body language was extremely incongruent with his professional role and exceptional height. He slouched in his chair when he sat. And when he stood upright, he wasn't conscious of his presence. Most of us are socially conditioned to look each other in the eye. Although my student looked at me when I spoke to him, he would look away when he spoke to me. It was clear that he thought he was being polite (as a tall man, he was vigilant about "not dominating"). Instead, this behavior made him seem timid, remote, and slightly disengaged.

Because he was more committed to detail than most people, he immediately took the principles of Vocal Power to heart. In our very first lesson, I called him over and over on his inability to maintain eye contact, continually bringing it into his conscious awareness. He has never averted his eyes once during subsequent lessons due to his intense discipline. I also taught him the concept of sitting in stature. By his second lesson, he embodied it perfectly. I have rarely seen individuals break their unconscious habits so rapidly.

Several lessons later, I demonstrated another secret of body language for my student. I wanted to show him that I could keep up with him during a walk down a corridor in his office even though I purposefully wasn't rushing—and in spite of my legs being shorter than his. My *modus operandi* was to carry myself in stature and elongate my stride to cover more territory, while he bustled down the hallway using extraneous energy and movements. As a result, I looked calm and composed, whereas he looked slightly harried and out of control. Because we timed ourselves and my way worked just as well as his, he understood that calmness under pressure was a more effective way of traveling by foot—and probably of doing other kinds of tasks. He also saw that it better conveyed the persona of the man he wanted to be: a dignified leader.

I felt extremely gratified when, after he tried walking down the corridor the same way I had, he commented on how much he enjoyed the feeling of staying conscious and walking in stature. It connected him to the sense of leadership he wanted to embody. It enabled him to tap into the core of his authentic Self—the hub of the Voice upon which I keep remarking. I have found that once people have tasted that sensation, they can *choose* to engage it consciously at every opportunity.

ACTIVITY:
Learning to Interpret
Your Body's Language

As the secret of Vocal Power lies in taking charge of both how you want to be and how you want to be known, it is vital to begin paying more attention to your body language. For until you become consciously aware of the signals you are "telegraphing" to the world, you cannot possibly choose new ones. Thankfully, the Vocal Awareness method provides an excellent framework within which to discover and make choices about the body.

Read through the following list of body language vocabulary and see how many behaviors apply to you. Among other possible habits, perhaps you:

- ♪ Fidget,
- ♪ Tap your toes,
- ♪ Drum your fingers,
- ♪ Avert your eyes,
- ♪ Have poor posture,
- ♪ Are clumsy,
- ♪ Jut out your hips,
- ♪ Chew on your lip,

♪ Fold your arms across your chest,

♪ Bite your fingernails,

♪ Hunch your shoulders,

♪ Point directly at people's faces,

♪ Rock back and forth on your heels,

♪ Slouch in your chair,

♪ Dip your head forward,

♪ Move stiffly and awkwardly.

Do you have any of these sorts of habits? (There are, of course, many more body language habits than these.) Were you unconscious of them until they were pointed out just now? This process is called the Vocal Awareness method because awareness is the first step in solving any problem. We can't solve a problem that we don't recognize.

Now, get out a piece of paper and a pen and make a personal "to do" list so you can work on eliminating those physical behaviors that don't adequately represent your new persona. Next, make a similar list of behaviors that would positively suit your persona and get ready to adopt them. Ask, "How can I *embody* leadership?" "How can I *embody* friendliness?" (Of course, use whatever is on the persona statement you wrote in Chapter 1.) How would a leader or friend sit, walk, speak on the telephone, or shake hands?

As you continue to practice the daily vocal workout, the empowerment rituals will become ever more deeply ingrained in your mind/body/spirit. And then they will find their way into your real life "performances," too. Working to improve your body language is a terrific way to bridge Vocal Awareness practice and everyday life. As you begin expressing your authentic Voice with greater frequency, the rituals will help you feel more secure and confident than you ever have before.

Up to now, you've been diffusing Vocal Power through various physical habits. Now, instead of chewing on a fingernail (or whatever it is that you do), you'll begin to *Love and Let Go*, or to *Allow a Silent, Loving, Down-through-your-body Breath*. Please understand: You may have to stop yourself and make a physical adjustment 8, 18, 80, or 800 times a day, yet each time you do it will be a victory.

ADDRESSING YOUR CHALLENGES

Standing or Sitting in Stature

When you're standing or sitting in stature, you should feel like your best Self: confident, dignified, valuable, sovereign, and so forth. But this is not a rigid position. I want you to be comfortable in your body.

That doesn't mean you always have to be perfectly upright. Remember: You're not trying to become someone who you are *not* but merely trying to bring who you really *are* out. Therefore, being "in stature"— whether you are standing, sitting, or walking—should not be a radical departure from what already feels comfortable to you, unless it is not serving you well.

So, we can sit in stature and at the same time put our arms up on the back of the sofa, lean on an elbow rest, have our feet up, or tuck a leg beneath us. What's important is to imagine a sensation, like the pull of a thread, lifting us up through the top of our heads. Sitting in this manner helps us breathe freely, remain conscious of our Self, and lift our upper torsos. It opens, releases, settles, and balances us—and it is a major tenet of Vocal Power. Be all you can be, claim your Self, starting here—starting now.

I recently had a client, a man in his early 30s, who was interested in meeting women socially. When I asked him to set up a role-playing scenario, he chose to pretend that he was in a singles bar. However, when he decided to sit in stature, it took him 90 seconds to two full minutes to stop giggling, get louder, and be comfortable. He was so unused to this way of being that it made him feel embarrassed, and he appeared uncomfortable. But the longer he practiced, the more this behavior dissipated.

My businessman student at the beginning of this chapter practiced being in stature while walking, standing, and sitting, and he told me it felt "wonderful." That's what is great about it. You'll like the feeling. Even though you may feel slightly embarrassed when you are learning new behavior or by your intentions (e.g., to meet women or men comfortably and honestly), it is the most natural posture there is, and it will ultimately feel more comfortable than standing, walking, or sitting the "old way."

You can always use the daily vocal workout to review how your body feels and looks when you assume a new posture, especially if you have the need to evaluate it because you feel awkward. In addition, if you feel vulnerable and exposed when you give up folding your arms in front of your body, slouching, and looking down (for instance), use the empowerment rituals to show yourself compassion and understanding while you are practicing and bringing the new posture into live "performance" situations.

The structure of the vocal workout is an invaluable support, particularly when you are still in the phase of the Work that I call the "talking your Self into it" stage. The best advice I can give right now is to surrender to the structure until its validity has been proven to you beyond a shadow of a doubt. Do your daily practice sessions even when you do not want to do them and be meticulous about following my instructions. Every aspect of the Vocal Awareness method serves a vital purpose within the structure.

Do not leave pieces out. "Sort of" doesn't count.

Standing in stature may feel odd at first, although you have found the right balancing point for your head. While looking in the mirror may inform you: "Good! You've got it!" at the same time, your kinesthetic awareness of your body may contradict: "Wrong! You're tilted, rigid, uneven, artificial," and so forth. Use the mirror. Your body is advising you based on its past holding patterns. Another thing that really helps people is that idea about a thread running along the spine and pulling them up through the crown of the head, no matter how they shift around. This image has movement and flexibility; it's not static.

Please be mindful. Be kind to yourself when you are looking in the mirror. Most of us share the tendency toward harsh self-judgment until we train ourselves otherwise. That's why *Love and Let Go* is such a powerful ritual. Go ahead and tell yourself out loud "I love you" several times a day. Act as though this statement is true and it ultimately will become true. One day, perhaps not long from now, you will hear yourself say it and you will believe it. Until then, fake it if you must because the alternative, to be candid, is less pleasant and supportive.

Lots of people have trouble standing in stature without rocking on their heels, shifting their weight from side to side, jutting out a hip, or assuming a position that I like to call "Adam's fig leaf." In this position, the hands are clasped in front of the genitals. It's an instinctive gesture of protection, of course. The point is that these behaviors rob you of Vocal Power. Visually, they tell the story that you may be ill at ease or anxious. Closed stances, such as the fig leaf or folding your arms across your chest, often send a message that you are defended, unavailable, and remote, especially if your facial expression does not counteract that impression. Of course, you may not be any of these things. They could just be someone's misinterpretations of how you feel.

In my group workshops, I like to do a show-and-tell wherein I ask students to call out adjectives to describe my attitude when I'm standing in a folded-arm posture. We do it twice and the only change I make is to switch from not smiling to subtly smiling. The first facial expression elicits words like irritable, defensive, and preoccupied, whereas the second garners relaxed, friendly, and comfortable. This demonstrates that body language is a complete picture rather than tiny pieces of separate information. And it also enhances awareness of the silent communication of meaning.

It is also noteworthy that different postures change the sound of our voices, which is a fact that's worth some experimentation to observe. Record your voice saying the same sentence in several different positions, including an open and uplifted posture of stature, and then assess its qualities. I believe you will discover for yourself that when you are standing or sitting in stature you sound more energized, clear, and dynamic. The difference you hear may be subtle, but your voice will definitely be enhanced.

ACTIVITY:
Being Comfortable While Standing

In this activity, I simply want you to stand with your feet together and your arms hanging freely at your sides. What does that feel like—awkward and vulnerable or confident and comfortable? Can you easily maintain your balance in this position? Are you unnecessarily tensing any of your muscles? Most people feel a little tentative when standing with their feet pressed together, as though a strong wind or a slight shove might knock them over.

Begin applying the principles of Vocal Awareness if you haven't already done so. How does that change the way you feel? Notice everything from your physical sensations to your mental and emotional responses.

Remain standing like this until you can embody the position in Vocal Power. Repeat the activity from time to time as a device for checking in.

Maintaining Eye Contact

Remember the adage "The eyes are the windows to the soul"? Well, it's true—or at least partially true. By averting your eyes, you rob people of an important communication tool. Eye contact gives us a tangible sensation of connection. It literally seems to magnify the energy behind any spoken communication. If this is your challenge, make a decision to come back into eye contact with whomever you are speaking as soon as you notice you've lost it. Consciously choose to self-correct constantly. A vital Vocal Awareness ritual is *Pay Attention/Deeper Listening.*

Use an audiotape recorder or a video camera to record yourself as you practice speaking and maintaining eye contact with your family and friends. Notice the subtle or not-so-subtle differences in how you sound. Your voice will probably be flatter, less resonant, and less energized when you are averting your eyes. Not only will you sound less animated but people will also perceive you that way.

Another way to practice eye contact is to focus your attention on something specific in a room and speak directly to it. Part of the issue is being able to maintain focus while communicating. At first blush, even this may seem unnerving. You may flutter your eyes and keep averting them frequently. But stick to it. Focus on your reflection in the mirror and observe your responses. Does this feel comfortable or confrontational? Does your head dip down? Does your body tense up in any area? Each step of the way, call the empowerment rituals to mind. Go back to breathing deeply and loving yourself.

When we do the Work, there may be times when we suddenly feel judgmental of the experience. We may feel arrogant or pretentious, like we're faking or too full of our Selves. These are critical, fearful thoughts about being exposed. The reason we feel unsafe is that the experience is unfamiliar. But I submit to you that being in Vocal Power is actually safer than not being in it. *Vocal Power puts us in charge of ourselves and enables us to make better, conscious choices.* Rather than abdicating our power to someone else or the circumstances around us, when we use the empowerment rituals, such as *Thank You to My Source* and *Love and Let Go*, we are waking up, changing our energy, and developing the ability to be sovereign over our Selves and, to the best of our abilities, our lives.

Freedom without direction is chaos. As we provide direction, we have the opportunity for creating life or art on our own terms.

Speaking on the Telephone

Due to the advances in communications technology, more people work out of their homes today using computers and telephones. Or, even if they have office careers, their cellular phones are practically welded on the side of their faces whenever they leave their desks. A phone is a typical business tool for handling sales, networking, and other kinds of transactions. Personally, I teach weekly phone sessions for students who live throughout the United States, Canada, and Europe even though I live in California. Being in Vocal Power while talking on the telephone is therefore of critical importance to me, as it will now become for you.

There's a practical success tip I would like to share with you. Post the Vocal Awareness Checklist and the Arc of Sound image next to your telephone where you can see them as you carry on your conversations. As the phone rings—and before you pick up the receiver— give yourself a moment to put yourself in Vocal Awareness and stand or sit in stature. *Thank* your *Source, Love and Let Go,* and *Allow a Silent, Loving, Down-through-*your-*body Breath.* Then answer the phone. Notice how this makes you feel.

Vocal Awareness Reminders

Placing abbreviations of the points on the Vocal Awareness Checklist in the margins of your presentations can be helpful. It's interesting how the mind/body/spirit understand what "L&LG" means, for instance. These reminders are discreet. No one will know what they mean except you.

S:	Stand or Sit in Stature;
TYMS:	*Thank You to My Source;*
L&LG:	*Love and Let Go;*
D/B:	*Allow a Silent, Loving, Down-through-my-body Breath;*
E/A:	*See the Nasal Edge and Arc of Sound;*
PADL:	*Pay Attention/Deeper Listening;*
T/T:	*Take My Time;*
C/S:	*Be Conscious of Self.*

Discover the power of these reminders for yourself. Write out a thought and add the abbreviation L&LG or D/B in front of it. Then read the sentence and notice what your body does. You'll see that inserting these in the text of speeches or of everyday memos in the workplace will help you remain focused and on target. If you are skeptical, just wait until you try it!

During phone conversations, be cognizant of releasing any tongue, jaw, neck, and shoulder tension. *Take Your Time.* Stay conscious and be in the ritual of *Pay Attention/Deeper Listening. See the Nasal Edge and Arc of Sound.* Ask your Self: "What's my persona?" Always go back to the persona statement you wrote in Chapter 1. In fact, post this, as well as the Checklist, near your phone. It can be helpful in reminding you to be there for your Self.

Having feedback is critically important to the learning process. Tape-record your side of phone conversations and review them later for developing Vocal Awareness. (Again, remember, of course, that it is not considerate to tape-record other people without their permission.) Use the second and third aspects of your daily vocal workout to plan the standard telephone moments, such as what you say when you first answer, any "pitches" you're supposed to use, as well as how to handle emotionally difficult moments, like breaking bad news or disagreeing on some points in a contract negotiation.

Vocal Power is impressive on the telephone. It has enabled me to bypass typical hiring processes more than once. In fact, I've landed several important jobs simply based on our phone conversations without meeting the people who were hiring me in person. These have included my workshop appearances at the Esalen Institute and my first audiotape/videotape publishing endeavor.

Many people use the telephone as a way to connect socially. In this fast-paced world we live in, we use the phone to maintain friendships and keep in contact with our loved ones during our business trips. Have you ever fallen in love with the sound of someone's "phone voice"? It happens a lot. Need I say more?

Greetings Matter

Okay, if you haven't figured it out by now, the advice in this book is not directed at being more *appropriate*; it's targeted at being and revealing your authentic Self. So, there isn't a specific formulaic way to greet people that you must learn in order to succeed at work or become popular. However, *underlying* any words of greeting that you do utter, I want you to *be* and also to *feel* conscious, honest, unpretentious, and comfortable.

Several years ago, an awkward appearing young man came to me for help. He was a computer programmer at the beginning of his career and desperately wanted to improve his speaking voice. To get the kind of job he wanted, he knew he had to impress an interviewer. He also needed to be able to work face-to-face with clients. He would have to gain their confidence and put them at ease if he was ever going to succeed. As we introduced ourselves, he pumped my hand mechanically, repeatedly blinked his eyes, and, in a shy and monotone voice, said, "Hello, my name is Roger." This simple interaction communicated volumes about his situation and my heart went out to him. He had so many problems. It was evident that he was inhibited, lacked social graces, and had little or no self-awareness. But I also knew that he had just taken an important step in the right direction. He had begun the journey to realize Vocal Power.

Roger and I met once a week over the course of the next several months. As his coach, I taught him how to present—share—himself from scratch: how to tuck in the front of his shirt so there were no wrinkles, how to line up the heels of his dress socks inside his shoes so they wouldn't bunch up or droop, how to stand in stature, how to shake hands and look people in the eye, and how to express his ideas. He worked on his own at home everyday, practicing the vocal workout religiously. He'd also keep a small tape recorder running in one of his jacket's side pockets when he went on job interviews so he could review his "performances" with me during our coaching sessions and on his own.

There's another important element of this story. Roger had struggled for years with clinical depression. He had several suicidal episodes and generally took strong mood-altering medications. After a few months of working together, I spoke on the telephone with his psychiatrist—with Roger's permission—and he informed me that Roger had substantially improved. Ever since he'd begun learning the Vocal Awareness method's strategies of caring for himself, he had no further suicidal episodes.

Although Roger represents an extreme, I never doubted his ultimate success. So although the process took time and his transformation didn't happen overnight, Roger did metamorphose like a butterfly hatching from a cocoon. After many—sometimes agonizing—job interviews, he finally got an offer for the position he sought. Two years later, he came back and we worked on additional vocal refinements using the same fundamental techniques. As a result, he got a promotion. Developing Vocal Power was the key to his career growth.

Explore shaking hands, introducing your Self, and saying "hello" to people. Strive to apply the rituals during each greeting. (Through commitment and practice, the awareness will very rapidly become organic to you—integrated—so it won't interrupt the flow of what you are doing.) It doesn't matter whether you're an assistant, a boss, a classroom teacher, or an artist. Go out into the world and observe your interactions. Notice if your behavior changes from situation to situation. Do you greet superiors differently from subordinates? Do you treat people in business differently from your friends? Notice whether you look down when you should be looking people directly in the eye. Do you pull your hand away too rapidly from a handshake? Is your grip too firm, too soft, or just right?

Don't just do the rituals and then slip into unconsciousness afterwards. Make a point each time to go to a deeper level of respect, conscious awareness, and presence. Every greeting (and every ensuing conversation) will hold a discovery for you. And believe it or not, the rituals will soon become ingrained so that their inclusion is simply the way a greeting goes. This can happen extremely rapidly if you are very purposeful and diligent. Remember: Greetings are one of the most important bonding rituals in our society.

After you've gathered enough information about your behavior, practice greeting people the way you like to be greeted. Ask your friends and family to be your "guinea pigs." Record yourself on videotape and watch it later. Is there anything that is short-circuiting communication? Perhaps an obstacle is as simple as wearing bracelets on your right wrist. In this case, push them up your arm before shaking hands so they don't get in the way, or remove them entirely. Find the solutions that empower you.

ACTIVITY:
Prove it to Your Self

Most people form an opinion in as little as three seconds. You included. So play this fun little game whenever you're meeting new people. As soon as possible after meeting, jot down your initial impressions of them (or make a purposeful mental note) and see how many conclusions you have jumped to on only a little evidence. Figuring out which presentational clues trigger specific impressions is information you can use. If you're forming impressions of others, others are likewise forming impressions of you.

YOUR GROOMING

Another reason I told you Roger's story was to reiterate the point that you need to work on every element of your Voice—the sounded voice, the voice in your head, your inner voice, and your body language, which includes the details of your physical appearance. People are most comfortable in the presence of those who take good care of and accept themselves. Your choice of appearance tells a story about your identity and character. Just as you learn to show your Self love and compassion by practicing the vocal workout, your grooming sends a message to the world about how much respect you feel you deserve. And please don't mistake this for your genetically determined "looks." I am not referring to the set of your eyes or the length of your nose.

"Grooming" is an umbrella term that encompasses showering, shaving, makeup, haircuts, and clothing. You might be surprised how often this comes up—or how easy it is to overlook. I had one successful business client who was a little bit sloppy and an especially terrible shaver. Often, his shirt wasn't tucked in properly. And he usually left whiskers on his cheek just below his jawline. He wasn't paying enough attention because he wanted to get the task done in a hurry, which was exactly the impression I had picked up. I reminded him that when he shaved, he had to shave *fully*. "Is this the same level of care you extend to your colleagues and clients?" I asked. He got the message.

People's appearances should suit their personas. They need the right clothes, the right eyeglasses, and the right haircuts. Oftentimes, I'll literally bring in an image stylist to work with my students directly. I have learned from these professionals that most of us require only a few good outfits hanging in our wardrobe closets. They become our *uniforms*. Once we learn what colors and designs suit us best, we are basically set for life, although it's worth reevaluating our images every so often. Personally, my hair went straight back for the majority of my adult life. But my eldest son, Isaac, who among other significant talents is a gifted fashion consultant, made an appointment for me with an excellent hairstylist who created a new cut. It totally changed my look and suits me better.

Taking the Next Step

There are many opportunities during the Vocal Power journey for us to get to know our deeper Selves more intimately. Maybe it seems superficial, therefore, to focus equal attention on facial expression, clothing, and other external characteristics. That's probably because we're habituated to believe that we are using appearance, mannerisms, and outward "stuff" to mask our flaws. From now on, I would like you to reframe this erroneous belief in terms of Vocal Awareness. Image is everything. But it begins with the image we have of our deeper Selves. Through Vocal Awareness, the deeper Self is then reflected in everything we do.

In these terms, our images reflect a higher truth and thereby reveal the magnificence of our identities and aspirations.

In the next chapter, we'll explore some of the ways we can use the Vocal Awareness method to support and nurture our Selves. This begins with a fundamental acknowledgment that even if we feel that no one *is* on our side, *we* must be on our side. It is the birthright of all human beings to expand their potentials, express themselves, enjoy life's abundance and pleasures, and make meaningful contributions to the community and world.

Believe in Your Self

*To be persuasive, we must be believable; to be believable,
we must be credible; to be credible, we must be truthful.*
—Edward R. Murrow

When we believe in our Selves, we are much more likely to take responsibility for the direction that our lives are taking. Self-acceptance and a sense of deserving seats us at the head of a table generously laden with delectable and nourishing dishes, where we're sovereigns feasting on life's abundance. The good news is that the distance between yearning for the life we are envisioning and actually leading that life usually can be traveled, *so long as we are willing to do what it takes.*

People frequently believe they are limited when actually they've just become habituated to leave out the steps that are necessary to succeed. I've even seen people in the business of helping others to succeed—knowledgeable folks, such as human resources managers, life coaches, and executive recruiters—fail to apply the same strategies for success that they recommend to their clients. Yet it's no wonder that many people don't (or can't) take steps, as they sometimes don't even know that there are various steps to take. The Vocal Awareness method reverses the tendency to Self-limit.

The Five Pillars of the Work that I've been teaching you in this book are:

♪ *Consciousness:* Become ever more aware of everything.

♪ *Vision:* Selectively imagine what you want in your life and who you want to be from this day forward. Then *commit* to that vision and take the journey one step at a time, both focusing on the moment and the path ahead.

♪ *Integrity:* Adhere to your daily vocal workouts and conscientiously apply the techniques of Vocal Awareness whenever and wherever possible in your everyday life. Be meticulous, precise, and consistent. Live in the integrity of the persona you've chosen to be. *Do not omit a single step no matter how seemingly insignificant it may be!*

♪ *Integration:* Twin to integrity, integration shares the same root source, meaning "wholeness." Notice and observe the subtle—and not so subtle—transformations filtering through your mind/body/spirit and into your life as a result of your persistent practice.

♪ *Mastery:* Enjoy a lifelong process of ever more fully realizing the depth, breadth, and potential gifts of your authentic Self—your being.

In this chapter, we're going to explore the positive ramifications of believing in your Self. Since you've read this far, my guess is that you've already been practicing the vocal workout for a few days or weeks. Therefore, you've certainly discovered an extraordinary well of resources deep within you, such as resilience, compassion, and enthusiasm, which impel you courageously forward. I am also certain that you've encountered some of your personal emotional "demons," as well as a number of other obstacles to improved communication and Self-mastery. I cannot encourage you strongly enough to continue to apply the Vocal Awareness method diligently in the face of these threats to your success. The Vocal Power journey is an ongoing process of bringing stumbling blocks out of the darkness and into the light of consciousness where they can no longer trip you up.

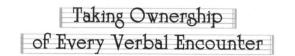

Taking Ownership
of Every Verbal Encounter

I once coached a high-ranking executive from a Fortune 500 company. She had a subordinate who constantly tried to intimidate her and defied her authority. In face-to-face encounters, this man would glare at her, crowd into her personal space, and use an aggressive, sarcastic tone. He openly challenged her decisions. He was a "vocal bully." This problem had really gotten out of hand and was disrupting her whole staff. My student told me she felt powerless in the office.

Here's the interesting part: My student had been the captain of the women's basketball team at a major university. A jock her entire life, she never felt intimidated on the court. While playing pickup basketball one weekend in a local park, a man on the sidelines started verbally hassling her. When he approached her in a threatening manner, she took the ball and threw it right at him. Even though he then took a swing at her, she didn't back down. That's how strong and courageous she could be. But she was afraid to embody that boldness and power when she was wearing a corporate uniform (a business suit) instead of a basketball uniform.

As we worked on building Vocal Power, among

other things, we delved into the issue of her identity. She addressed her fears about not "fitting in" or "making waves" and wrote a persona statement that included being capable, confident, and a "captain of industry." We orchestrated a conference between her and her subordinate. The purpose of this meeting was to put him in his place. Then we decided what she was going to say and wear, how she would stand and sit, and the layout of the room. She used the Vocal Awareness techniques to prepare. As a result, she felt commanding, *safe*, and was in Vocal Power when the encounter took place a few days later. Once the subordinate understood the reality that he couldn't push her around anymore, he apologized and took responsibility for his actions. He quit his job soon after. My student has since moved on herself and is now the chief executive officer of another company.

Believing in your Self can equate to remaining calm, cool, and collected in confrontational situations where you need to stand up for a principle or your own human dignity. But it's not about tricking other people or manipulating them. It is about giving your Self permission to be who you are and to communicate from that point of view as consciously, truthfully, clearly, and effectively as possible.

I designed the following "leadership statement" for one of my corporate clients. It applies to anyone who chooses to be in Vocal Power. See if you are now ready to make the same two commitments:

♪ In the essence of every discussion, I will consciously convey authority, vision, wisdom, and attention to detail.

♪ In every communication, I will consciously convey and maximize the full potential of my persona.

Developing Vocal Power enabled my student to handle her troublesome subordinate effectively by giving her the means to claim ownership of their encounters. By applying the Vocal Awareness techniques beforehand, she also learned how to show emotional support for her Self. But her transformation went much deeper than a single relationship with a colleague. Like putting on a new pair of shoes, she stepped into the authentic truth of her persona by establishing a vision for her best life and following through on it. In the activity below, you will prepare to take a similar step.

ACTIVITY:
Writing Your Vision Statement

Imagine that you were visiting an unfamiliar city and wanted to go to a specific store. Left to your own devices, you might wander the streets randomly and never find your way. But with a map in hand, you could get there on your first attempt. Having a map saves you both time and effort and improves your chances for success. Similarly, once you have chosen your new persona, it is important to get clear about what that would look like in tangible, practical terms. Your vision statement is another piece of the Vocal Power map. In this activity, you will begin to determine your life's purpose.

First, draft some ideas on paper about the purpose for which you are dedicating your life. Your vision statement is a written declaration of your reason for being. A rule of thumb is to dream big. We each create our own reality: If you dream small dreams, you're limiting your potential. What if you don't know your purpose? Don't worry. Just think about it for now—everyone must return often to address that issue afresh.

Please understand that it may not be possible to write your statement down perfectly at first. It will most likely change and mature as you do. Among other things, it will possibly become shorter and more specific. Later on, read it regularly and memorize it if you can. As an example, my personal vision statement in part reads, "To help all those with whom I work to achieve their own enlightenment and enjoy their own empowerment . . . also to help change the world through Voice."

ACTIVITY:
Writing Your Goals

An important follow-up to Writing Your Vision Statement is writing down your goals for achieving this vision. You need to be specific about how you can realize it. In my case, these goals include, in part, coaching sessions with individual students and clients, conducting corporate workshops, giving public lectures and classes, recording audiotapes and videotapes, and writing this book.

As you draft your goals, it is exceedingly helpful to frame them along a timeline. If you are looking for a job, for instance, commit to mailing your resumés on Thursday and making phone calls on Monday. Set daily, weekly, monthly, and yearly goals. If you know where you plan to be six months from now, it is much easier to imagine where you need to be in four months and two months, working backwards to get there. This helps make your goals easier to achieve, realistic, and attainable rather than idealistic. At the same time, keep your focus on the highest ideals of your vision statement, which is your lodestar.

Here is an example of a realistic goal: If your vision is to lose 30 pounds, it's realistic to assume that you can lose two pounds a week following a healthful diet and exercise regimen. Here is an example of an unrealistic goal: If your vision is to lose 30 pounds, it's unrealistic to assume you can do it in one month, no matter what you eat or how much you exercise. Even if you could, this would make you sick. And that's not an appropriate outcome.

Stick to the attainable, and be specific about it. Sociologists have determined that going to the supermarket with a shopping list saves us both time and money. If making a list is a good strategy for shopping, why not for life? Writing down your vision statement and goals will help connect them to the multidimensional reality of your life as you begin your journey to Vocal Power.

A timeline for an independent consultant seeking to attract more business and enhance his professional reputation by developing a Website as a marketing tool might look like this:

PURPOSE: DEVELOP A WEBSITE AS A MARKETING TOOL
TIMELINE: TWO MONTHS

Week 1:

♪ Establish a budget.

♪ Reread your persona statement (see Chapter 1).

♪ Interview Web designers and view their work.

♪ Determine how the process works, and explain professional needs and expectations.

♪ Make hire.

Week 2:

♪ Define specific elements to be included on the Website (e.g., services, resumé, photo-graphs, artwork, guest book, contact info, greetings, and testimonials).

♪ Purchase virtual domain.

♪ Schedule session with a photographer and/or illustrator.

Week 3:

♪ Approve basic Web design.

♪ Begin writing and delivering content (text) as requested by Web designer.

♪ Choose clothing, makeup, and accessories for photo shoot.

♪ Trim hair.

Week 4:

♪ Write and deliver more content to Web designer.

♪ Review the designer's progress and make corrections.

♪ Attend photo shoot.

♪ Review illustrator's progress.

Week 5:

♪ Write and deliver more content.

♪ Review further progress.

♪ Review photographer's contact sheets and make selections.

♪ Pick up artwork.

Week 6:

♪ Deliver photographs and illustrations to the Web designer.

♪ Also, more content.

Week 7:

♪ Make sure content, photos, and artwork are finalized on the Website.

♪ Have an extra pair of eyes look at it.

♪ Ask designer to make any corrections.

♪ Post the site.

Week 8:

♪ Invite past clients, members of mailing list, friends, and family—all "warm contacts"— to visit the site.

♪ Make sure it is listed on business cards, letterhead, and so forth.

I have found that one of the things most people don't do is allow for enough preparation time. If you're going to a meeting of any kind, for instance, you need to build enough time into your schedule to evaluate the material that's on the agenda. For this particular project, there were really three tracks that the independent consultant had to follow: 1) written material, 2) visual images, and 3) interfacing with the Web designer. Some people add musical compositions to their Websites, so this project could have been even more involved. This timeline helped get the job done properly.

By writing a timeline, you are creating a contract (with your Self) that has a structure and deadline. The following success tips will help you fulfill the bargain:

- ♪ Don't bite off more than you can chew. Set aside enough time.

- ♪ Be specific. That's the source of your structure.

- ♪ Write your plan down in your calendar or Palm Pilot—it can't only be mental.

- ♪ Honor your commitments! If you say you were going to do something on Tuesday and it's 9:00 P.M., then you have work to do before bedtime. Midterms took place on a certain day in school, and whether you were prepared, they happened anyway. In the same way, your plan must take place on the days you have allotted for the whole structure to succeed.

Get Ready for Your Defining Moment

As I mentioned in Chapter 1, the movie *Annie* was a pivotal project in my professional teaching career, leading to many more opportunities. But the job wasn't handed to me on a silver platter; I had to go after it. Because I had committed my Self to a vision for my future, I was ready for this defining moment or another like it to occur. Yet if I hadn't anticipated the possibility, it might have passed me by. It was only my Self-awareness and belief in my ability to get the job well done that enabled me to persist in the face of obstacles.

You see, I had the opportunity first to work with Sean Connery, who was originally slated to play Daddy Warbucks in *Annie*, and then to work with Albert Finney, who ultimately played the role. Yet even though Albert and I worked together for over two years in preparation, I was not invited to go on location to New York City with the film company when shooting began. I had made several phone calls to no avail. But my inner voice told me to try once more. The line producer I spoke with explained in this conversation that the issue was the budget. They didn't believe enough in my work or, frankly, in me, to want to assume the cost of my services on an extended daily basis.

It didn't matter what they believed, however. I had been preparing myself for years to jump on this golden opportunity. After long hours of faithful Vocal Awareness training, I believed in my Self and knew the importance of remaining involved in the project and proving my abilities. Contributing to this particular movie could establish my professional reputation at a higher level and therefore bring me greater personal fulfillment, income, and career choices.

Nonetheless, I was faced with a dilemma: Was I going to let the size of the paycheck stand in my way when so many other intangible rewards might become available to me? I listened to my inner guidance and told the line producer: "I'll pay my way to New York. I won't take a per diem. I'll stay in my cousin's apartment. And I'll also discount my rate." This was simply too good an offer for them to refuse. So I got the job— and I have never regretted it. I made valuable relationships, I earned the money I needed, and I even got a screen credit.

Reading this, some readers might think that I "prostituted" myself to get the job on *Annie*. That I gave away too much. You may be wondering about my integrity. But I see events differently. Before the movie came along, I had already envisioned greater artistic and personal fulfillment—even opportunities like that one—so *the risk I took was required.* I trusted that everything was going to turn out well because I trusted my Self and my ability to respond to my circumstances. Finally, I also trusted that God would take care of me.

Everyone of us can use the Vocal Awareness method to prepare for our defining moments, those remarkable chances that suddenly arise when a dream is briefly within grasp. Such moments test our resolve:

Will fear and Self-doubt rule the day? Or will we seize the opportunity to launch ourselves into a future where we are transformed?

Often I find myself repeating a line from the movie *Apollo 13*: "Failure is not an option."

The line is said because several astronauts are stuck inside a malfunctioning capsule that's heading back to Earth with one shot at reentering the atmosphere. Shouldn't we all live our lives with as much commitment as they did in that moment? Or should we simply live on our own terms to the best of our abilities? If you personally want to strive for greatness, do so. But remember that you must envision that greatness clearly, and then take appropriate steps to achieve the vision.

Two of my students are currently taking career "leaps," relying upon their resources and integrity to give them wings. One is an athlete launching a movie career. The other is a former executive launching her own consulting business. Their role is to figure out what they need to do and then to be meticulous about doing it. My role as their communication strategist and life coach is to guide them to understand the dictates of their dreams—and then to nag them mercilessly (wink-wink). As they exemplify how we must unite tenacity and talent in order to realize our authentic Selves, I will include their stories below.

By the way, a defining moment is only *defining* if we are transformed afterwards. If a door opens up, but we do not walk through it into the passageway beyond, we have not taken the journey that was offered. But please understand that we can also be transformed by not walking through an open door. That, too, can define our lives and ourselves. The moments I am referring to here are pivotal moments. We all need to follow-up on the doors that open for us. Applying the Vocal Awareness techniques makes this less frightening and helps support us to take our defining steps.

Uniting Timing, Talent, and Tenacity

Over the years, I've observed that successful athletes, artists, politicians, and heads of corporations do their jobs more intensely than the rest of us do ours. Tenacity is one of the most important qualities in their success. But don't judge yourself unfavorably in comparison. Most of us were never taught to dedicate our Selves to a discipline. Reading this book may be the first exposure you've had to a structure that teaches you how to dedicate yourself to any kind of pursuit. Congratulations are in order. If you show up on a daily basis and do the Work as it is described in this book, the Vocal Power journey will teach you tenacity.

I don't spend much time worrying about talent. Obviously people possess different talents, but everyone has talents that can be developed. Instead, I advise my clients to focus on expanding their current abilities. *Strive for excellence rather than perfection.* Begin by dancing a simple two-step rather than doing the tango. Begin by swimming a lap rather than a mile. Concentrate on playing scales fluidly on the piano before you get out the sheet music for a concerto. Set the "bar" higher for yourself than it is right now, but don't elevate it to an impossibly high standard. That would merely set you up for defeat and disappointment. However, as you improve your abilities, revisit your standard and raise the "bar" again.

Keep in mind that there is a huge difference between *settling for* and *accepting* the level at which you're functioning at present. Settling is giving up, whereas acceptance is an absolute requirement if you want to improve your capabilities and do more. After acceptance, you move on and through any obstacles toward fulfillment.

Right now, make a decision to stop being concerned about how perfect you are *not* and to become more concerned about accepting your Self as imperfectly as you are. After all, who gets to define human "perfection"? Me? You? The neighbors? Our seeming imperfections are the qualities that give us our individuality. I passionately believe that we are meant to be different from one another.

My student, Franco Carlotto, is a bodybuilder from Zurich, Switzerland. He has held the title as Mr. World Fitness four times and, at the moment of this writing, is ranked as "the fittest man in the world" by the World Fitness Federation. As I mentioned a few pages back, he's beginning a movie career. In Europe, he was a successful spokesperson—a big fish in a small pond—but he took the risk to come to the United States, where, at least for a while, he'll be a small fish in a big pond. One of the questions he and I are confronting together is: How do you get over the hurdle?

The 29-year-old Franco is like a young Arnold Schwarzenegger. He and I work on his language skills, as his original languages are Swiss-German and Italian. But not just on articulation, as we're not shooting for him to sound like an American. He's European and that's a significant part of his identity. He wants to portray himself in a particular persona that's bigger, stronger, and more demonstrative, and a bit cleaner in his accent. Because he's a champion, I know I can be tough on him. I say, "I refuse to let you use a soft, shy, 'young' way of speaking. Speak as a champion—the way you designed your persona. And I'm not going to cut you any slack. How would you train yourself in the gym in the final month before a competition? Well, I want you to do your Vocal Awareness practices and sessions with me just as rigorously." He understands what that means, and he respects it because he would train someone in the gym the same way.

The second student I would like to tell you about is a former vice president of human resources at a major corporation. We've been working together off and on for about five years, and she has finally decided to hang her own shingle as a consultant. Last year, she left her original position to become the head of HR at a smaller firm (a big fish in a smaller pond), but it wasn't the right fit for her. She called me to help her chart her course over the next six-months and make the leap successfully. Like Franco, the question is: How do you get over the next hurdle?

My friend and I met for breakfast and we had established a clear timeline for her new business enterprise in only an hour. We devised a mission statement, set goals, outlined networking possibilities and a business structure, and made a list of products she would develop. In terms of Vocal Power, she realized her leap was to go out into the world and convey her identity as her Self, rather than the representative of another entity. She had to learn to hold onto the power of that identity and find her security in it.

Because my client was worried that she wouldn't have enough time to "get it all done," one of the activities she did before our next session, which I highly recommend you do as well, is called *Track Your Next 168 Hours*. (That's the number of hours in one week. It's not complicated.) Like most people, my client had never been 100 percent responsible for setting her own daily agenda.

ACTIVITY:
Track Your Next 168 Hours

As kids, we're made to attend school and so are given schedules. When we grow up, most of us go out and get jobs, and someone else tells us what to do. Therefore, it's important to find out where our time is spent during a real week.

To do this activity, you record every single thing you do for a 168-hour period, from sleeping to working, to grooming, to bill paying, to shopping, to dating, to watching TV. Only then can you decide for your Self what you can accomplish within reason on a daily and weekly basis. This helps you recognize and reorganize your use of time.

My friend Stephanie is a writer and she often finds herself on exceedingly short deadlines of a day or two. She's emotionally prepared to spend as many hours as necessary working on delivering her projects. But she simply cannot comply physically. After eight hours seated in front of her desk, she finds that her neck and back usually ache, her eyes glaze over, and her legs get stiff. She also gets a little bit lonely. So to continue working beyond that point offers diminishing returns. Therefore, her 168-hour plan has to include time for physical activity, such as walks outdoors, human contact, and plenty of rest. But by keeping a record, she has discovered that she formerly wasted time by remaining at her desk in front of her computer and working ineffectively, rather than tending to her needs. In a reality-based 24-hour period, she can write for eight hours, sleep for eight hours, and has an additional eight hours to do work away from her desk and/or manage other areas of her life, such as her relationships, laundry, grocery shopping, errands, and exercise.

Some people who do this activity discover that they've got 172 hours worth of stuff to do, even though there's only 168 hours to do it in. One client of mine was a salesman who was working 102 hours a week, despite having a wife and two small children at home. Tracking his time made him realize how skewed his priorities were. Another student looked clearly at the amount of time she spent commuting to work each morning and evening. Three hours a day multiplied by five days a week came to 15 hours! Within a few months, she sold her house and moved closer to her office. Now her commute is ten minutes each way, so she essentially bought herself 14 hours to pursue other interests.

Structure does not impinge. It liberates.

Once you've defined and reorganized your schedule, I recommend that you go back and look at your timeline again. Maybe you have a more realistic vision now.

Confronting Your "Demons"

As you begin to examine your Self and your persona and make the adjustments that Self-examination inevitably stimulates, you will find that the negative, repressive forces that live deep inside you—and that are used to being in charge—may rise up to the surface to scare you, threaten you, and confuse you. For whatever reason, those forces want to keep you from truly emerging into your greatness. Be wary of the huge *inner critic* that may come up trying to discourage you by saying things, such as "This is phony. This is not you.

Don't believe that you can do this."

When the inner critic comes up, you have to respond, "I believe in my Self and I'll do my very best!" even if you doubt it. After all, doing your best is all that any of us can ever do, isn't it? As I've said before, there's always a stage in the Vocal Awareness process where we're talking ourselves into it. (*It* being the persona, the behavior, the vision, and so forth.) Taking the time to respond to the negative voices in our heads and do our best is what counts. Not our doubts.

None of us got where we are today unscathed. We all have wounds of one kind or another and we need to be compassionate with our Selves, as well as commanding and structured. We have to hold ourselves on course and persevere in order to realize our dreams and meet our goals. But we also have to be available, kind, loving, and accepting, even when it seems that the world is not. The story below demonstrates how the Vocal Awareness method is a framework within which this can happen.

I once had a female student who, aside from being a lawyer and a prominent professional in her field, was also intensely dedicated to her personal growth. She had traveled widely, skydived, and even fire-walked at Tony Robbins' seminars. You would never have described her as "fearful." We had spoken on the telephone and I found her to be a charming, honest, and intellectually rigorous individual. Our first face-to-face session took place in Washington, D.C., about ten days before she was scheduled to deliver a presentation to a thousand trial attorneys. Right away, I observed that her jaw was extremely tight, her breath was inhibited, and her voice was shallow and pitched very high. As we continued, I soon discovered that she was almost completely out of touch with her body and emotions. She demonstrated many nonverbal signs of unconscious avoidance that led me to believe that she'd been deeply traumatized in the past.

A few days later, she flew out to Los Angeles for another coaching session. After about twenty minutes, I stopped my student and gently asked when she had been harmed—and also whether it would be all right to talk about it. Although she was initially surprised, she courageously told me that she had been brutally raped 15 years earlier. Her attacker had hurt her so severely that he broke a number of her ribs and then he left her lying injured outdoors in a snowbank. Until the moment we spoke about it, she had never told anyone what had happened before except for her attending physician.

For the remainder of that session and in future ones, we explored how her strong sense of needing to protect herself had been subconsciously affecting her Voice. As we worked to prepare her for her speech that day, she realized that on a certain level she perceived the people she was about to address as her potential attackers. I helped her understand how she could use the structure of the Vocal Awareness method to begin to feel safe again. Her conscious daily commitment to Self-nurturing and her meticulous adherence to the Vocal Awareness workout ultimately calmed her nervous system and made her feel safer and more confident. These techniques enabled her to confront her anxiety, deal with it, and ultimately move through and eliminate it. By accepting and acknowledging her trauma and allowing it to surface in the presence of her own compassion, she created an opportunity to release her pain and liberate her authentic Voice.

I assure you that in time, my remarkable friend and client went on to become a meaningful and significant public speaker. So can you—if that is your goal. She also underwent a deeper transformation. Her dedication to the task of developing her Voice impacted her life on many levels, not only in speaking. It became a metaphor for her Self-esteem and empowerment in her personal relationships and on the job. And, as you can see, and perhaps have already experienced for your Self, the process of developing Vocal Awareness is intimate, often delicate, and powerful. Thus, it is essential to create an emotionally and spiritually safe space to do your work—a holy place—especially when you are confronting your most persistent demons.

The Latin root of the word intimate is *intimus*, meaning "intrinsic" or "essential."

If you are interested in developing a more intimate relationship with your deeper Self and experiencing greater emotional freedom, do the following activity.

ACTIVITY:
Writing from Both Sides of the Brain

This activity is not as much a vocal and auditory exercise as it is a spiritual and mental pursuit. I have my students do it when they need to commune with their subconscious minds and reveal new insights on what makes them tick or holds them back. The hemispheres of the human brain work in tandem, yet they perceive and process our experiences differently and govern complementary abilities. The *left brain* is considered logical, mathematical, and linear. The *right brain* is considered emotional, verbal, and associative. So, as we stimulate these capacities by alternately writing with our dominant and nondominant hands, in essence we are able to *speak* with different parts of our Selves.

Begin by taking out a pen and a clean pad of paper. With your dominant hand (for the majority of people, this means the right hand), write down a word or name from the following list of suggestions (feel free also to improvise using your own words):

♪ Beauty		♪ Sexuality	
♪ Vision		♪ Courage	
♪ Power		♪ Pain	
♪ Anger		♪ Self	
♪ Joy		♪ Value	
♪ Love		♪ Integrity	
♪ Passion		♪ Parents' names	
♪ Commitment		♪ Names of siblings	
♪ Sensuality			

Next, using your nondominant hand, write in a stream of consciousness about that word or name and what it means to you. Keep going until you have nothing left to contribute to the topic. Remember: There is no "right" or "wrong" idea or feeling, sentence structure and length don't matter, and neat handwriting is not an issue. This is "Top Secret," for your eyes only. Sometimes memories come up, sometimes fantasies, sometimes pictures, sounds, or even smells. Follow the flow without censoring yourself.

The third step is to take what you learn from your writing and integrate it into your persona. You may have been given significant messages from the part of your mind that usually lingers just below your conscious awareness. It is important to listen. So, in your daily training sessions, apply the Vocal Awareness techniques to the words and information you've learned. I believe this activity will inspire you.

Integration and Self-Mastery

As a young man, my student and friend, Hans Li, played the piano, the violin, and sang. Then he became an accomplished architect. Today, a few decades later, he is a fine arts photographer and leads an enlightened artist's life. He has made the commitment to awaken creatively. About a year and a half ago, he began to open his Voice as a singer using the Vocal Awareness techniques. You see, even with the liberation of his voice, he could never access it in the way he wanted. It just didn't feel free to him. Because he wasn't content with that subtle distinction and was willing to do what it took to develop his gifts, I consider him a person who approaches his life in a Self-mastered way.

After we began working together, we soon found

ourselves going to the recording studio every time I was in New York. Among other things, we recorded poems about the gods of the north, south, east, and west based on shamanic concepts. One idea led to another and we started improvising. For one take, he made up words. For subsequent ones, he said the same phrase—one take using a high voice—one take using a low voice. Then in editing we layered the different takes together like a choir.

One of the things I most liked about this approach was that it incorporated the so-called *masculine* and *feminine* aspects of Hans' voice. Vocal Awareness goes beyond social stereotypes and seeks to develop what I call the "androgynous voice," the balanced expression of the male and female qualities in a fulfilled individual—the integrated, whole Self. More recently, we've been recording chants. Overall, the process has been extraordinarily liberating for both of us. And I have especially enjoyed working with Hans because we're focusing on aesthetic qualities in minute detail.

In one Vocal Awareness lesson, I took out a legal pad and had Hans draw a horizontal line, anticipating that the results would reveal subtle knowledge about awareness and focus. Then I had him do it again "as an artist" while using the empowerment rituals. Because of his architectural background, this produced a strong impact. What fascinated me most was that as the pencil was moving across the page, it was rotating between his thumb and index finger. I asked him why, and he told me the story of his first art class at Harvard University. The professor had said, "For the next three hours you'll draw horizontal lines only." In the second class, the professor had the students draw only vertical lines. It was an enormously structured, meticulous, and patient process of learning and integration. As a result, some 25 years later, whenever Hans draws lines, he is wholly embodied in them.

Afterwards, we spent 45 minutes practicing one note, exploring as many permutations of it as we could from the release of Hans' jaw, to the sensuality of the tone, to the way he used his lips, and the positions of his neck and shoulders. I wanted him to embody the full expression of this tone in the same way he drew a single line on a page, so that it wouldn't just be a sound but would maximize its aesthetic representation. Therefore, he could feel and listen to the note the way he had been trained to observe lines.

ACTIVITY:
Drawing Lines and Circles

I highly recommend that you spend time on your own doing the same activity Hans did. It has two parts. Get a pad of paper and a pencil.

Begin by drawing straight lines and circles casually for as long as you want. Notice how you feel.

Then, on a separate piece of paper, draw more lines and circles using the Vocal Awareness techniques. Stand or sit in stature. Apply the empowerment rituals. Allow a deep and loving breath. Release your tension. Explore the process of drawing beautiful, sensual images. And then stay conscious and aware while you do so.

Use this activity to discover what it feels like to focus so precisely on one task. If Vocal Awareness can enhance the process of drawing circles and lines, just imagine what it can do for the rest of your life.

Claim Your Self

I want you to be Self-mastered, whether you are practicing your daily Vocal Awareness vocal workout, doing the functions of your job or chores around your house, or you're involved in every different kind of relationship. I promise you that when you consciously retrace the Vocal Awareness rituals *every single time you do anything*, they will soon become fully integrated into your persona. From then on, you'll embody them. Period!

None of us lives in a vacuum. Life always provides new opportunities and experiences that expand us and our abilities. There are always going to be deeper levels of listening—being both cognizant and attentive to detail—and new arenas in which to apply the skills of Vocal Awareness.

Do you recall my friend Stephanie who was working on managing her weekly schedule? In a phone session, after I asked her to allow a loving breath and *Love and Let Go*, she said, "It made me feel more real." But I couldn't hear the passion in her voice. She had distanced herself from what she was saying, right in the middle of her sentence. She judged my possible response to it and vocally "backed off" the thought.

I had her repeat it, while paying particular attention to the punctuation. "Use an exclamation point! Let your voice drop down at the end. Visualize the words (which I had her write down) underlined in front of you," I told her. These are techniques I use a lot. I always *see* the words I'm saying in my mind's eye in front of me. And I *read* the punctuation!

Stephanie said the sentence two more times with stronger emphasis, more fully claiming her Self along the way. And finally she observed, "It's interesting that when I'm alone doing the Vocal Awareness techniques I never feel apologetic about it. It's only when another person enters the scene that I retreat that way." Right! *And she wouldn't have made that discovery if she hadn't noticed what she was doing and returned to the moment. She* had to be willing to stop and hold herself to a higher standard. Stepping back into her idea and expression—"It made me feel more real!"—was the next step in her Vocal Power journey.

Taking the Next Step to Mastery

Mastery is the intent to love everything you do as a reflection of your authentic Self. It is your passion that is truly meaningful in your life and to others. If you make the commitment to being Self-mastered, you will find, as Hans and my other students have found, that the journey of awareness deepens continually. As a result, they experience even more creativity in their lives. They experience more pleasure and beauty. Ultimately, the freedom they are seeking in opening their mouths and expressing their authentic Voices is matched by the freedom they are seeking in their lives.

In the next chapter, we're going to talk about accessing joy and freedom through the art of singing. There is nothing that compares to communing with your Self in song. It is perhaps the fastest and deepest means of finding, being in touch with, and revealing our passion.

8 Singing–The Power and the Pleasure

If you cannot teach me to fly, teach me to sing.
—Sir James Matthew Barrie

In all my travels around the world, I have never met anyone who didn't want to sing. Sometimes people tell me: "Unfortunately, I'm 'tone deaf,'" or "But I'm afraid to sing." Even so, everyone says, "If I had the chance, I would love to sing." The good news is that everyone can sing—and, with practice, sing well. We are born with this ability. In fact, singing is so intrinsically human that newborn infants will often hum as they nurse. They express their joy and satisfaction in the most fundamental way possible. Singing is not an outgrowth of speech as you might imagine; it actually uses distinct neural pathways. This is why our expressions are predominantly nonverbal when we tap into our deepest emotions. We keen, wail, moan, and sustain sound, for instance, when we are grieving.

An interesting correlation has been made between music and other forms of artistic expression. Hundreds of thousands of years ago, the earliest human beings learned the power of song. Today, archaeologists have discovered that the prehistoric caverns with the most masterfully created paintings on their walls are those with the best acoustical properties. Singing stimulates the entire mind/body/spirit.

The act of singing is natural. The art of singing is skill.

Singing is my passion and I hope to impart my enthusiasm to you in this chapter. By far, the best reason to sing is for the pure joy of it. Sound vibrations feel good. They are relaxing—even healing. They connect us to the depths of our emotions and to our spiritual Selves. Singing is a significant piece of the Vocal Awareness method. I teach many singing students, but I also teach many clients who come to me for help in developing Vocal Power for business to sing. Everyone benefits. Therefore, I can confidently promise you that you can learn to sing as magnificently as you have ever dreamed possible. Even if you don't think you can, I assure you that before you finish you'll be able to sing. If you're already a polished professional singer, the Vocal Awareness method will make you an even better singer.

There Is No Such Thing as "Tone Deaf"ness

We all can learn to sing if we have the patience to find our keys. My singing student Eve is proof of this. When I first met her, she thought she was "tone deaf" because she had tried to sing without success. It took three lessons just for her to be able to replicate and hold one tone. When she did, she began sobbing. It was terrifying for her to make a sustained sound. For three months, I'd have to find the pitch on my piano keyboard that she was making and ask her to sustain it. She couldn't find the notes I played. Then we'd go up by half steps—with a great deal of sobbing in between—losing the pitch as often as we found it. Finally, after months of diligence, she began singing "Home on the Range" in her daily practice sessions using the Vocal Awareness singing workout that you'll learn later in the chapter. She got a small electric keyboard to help her pick out the right notes.

Six months later, the next step was to have her mimic me while singing *a capella*—i.e., without accompaniment. I'd sing a phrase in her octave and then she'd sing the same phrase. When I asked her to sing along with me, we discovered she could now stay in tune. We had finally moved from rote learning to music making, and she could begin to express her Self. It was a huge milestone. There was emotion and vibrato in Eve's singing, and there was no more crying. In fact, she was often giggling during our lessons because it was so exhilarating to feel her own expression.

I reiterate: Even though it can take awhile, and you may need someone to work with you, there's no such thing as "tone deafness." You simply have to find the appropriate process and apply yourself meticulously. It requires willingness and patience.

When he was a teenager, I took my younger son, Eli, whitewater rafting. As we came around one bend into a little bit of flat water, there was an enormous granite boulder in front of us—cracked in half. A tree shoot was growing *through* it. And I couldn't help but marvel: How many millions of years may it had taken this tiny twig to crack open this gigantic boulder, seeking light? The patience of nature is extraordinary. That's the same fortitude we need to adopt in the pursuit of life—and the pursuit of singing. *With patience and persistence, we can triumph over any obstacles along the path.*

I get very angry when I hear scientists speak about poor pitch discrimination as "tone deafness" because I believe they may base their research on faulty premises. Joe Palca gave a report on National Public Radio's *All Things Considered*[2] that infuriated me. A Canadian psychologist had tested a woman and found that she needed to hear two computer generated tones four

2 January 16, 2002.

times, instead of once, in order to discriminate which was higher or lower. The conclusion was that it would be hopeless to teach her. But I see an opportunity there. So what if it takes longer? Her narrow ability could be expanded.

It seems to me that some scientists are more interested in controlling their studies so they can achieve clear results than in actually helping people to sing. We don't even know if the researchers are competent singers themselves. Pathologists don't always grasp the concept of vocal art, as they often think of voice as a mechanism rather than an instrument. Are they, perhaps, not the best judges of the process? *Please do not give away your power to limited belief systems.*

When I was teaching at the University of Southern California, I had a deaf student in my class. She couldn't even hear a tape recorder. At the end of the first semester, she sang phrases from the song "Do Re Mi" from *The Sound of Music* in tune, holding one hand on the top of an upright piano to feel its vibration and one hand on my throat feeling the vibration from my larynx. Because I sang with her and banged the notes out very loudly, she could feel the vibration. She could also read my lips. At the end of the second semester, with more work and extraordinary dedication, she sang the entire song "My Favorite Things" from the same musical from the center of the Bing Auditorium stage at USC—in tune.

This student missed the next semester, and returned for the following one, now singing a country western tune popular at the time, "Blue Bayou," at a performance level. You never would have known she had a hearing challenge. And, frankly, some people who think they are "tone deaf" have more trouble than this dedicated student of mine did. So, as you can see from the example of this conscious student, we all choose to be empowered or disempowered in allowing or disallowing ourselves to do things.

Why Do Some People Sound Better Than Others?

When you buy a compact disc of your favorite singer, you're buying a recording that might have cost a quarter of a million dollars to produce. It wasn't done with a Dixie cup and string. It is important to recognize this truth. When you record your own voice, don't expect it to sound like an expensive CD. And if you record it in the living room or bedroom, don't expect it to sound like it did in the bathroom. Wherever you are, it's going to sound different. You can never recreate the "bathroom sound" anywhere else.

Since we are born with the desire to sing, everyone likes to do it, whether we think we do it well. Those who think we are good singers, do it often, whereas the more self-conscious among us probably only sing when nobody is around. Singing more frequently helps us improve. Among other things, our muscles get stronger that way.

But at this point, I don't want you to worry about whether you sound "good" or "bad." Don't judge it. Don't compare yourself with other people. Instead, I want you to sing solely for your Self. As you learn Vocal Awareness, I want you to listen very deeply to your inner voice and to tune out those old mental tapes that say, "Ick, you can't sing." Switch off messages you get, such as "I have to present my song for someone's approval." Even people with phenomenal voices can be self-critical. For instance, I taught a well-known Broadway and film actress who used to turn and face upstage (away from the audience) whenever she auditioned because she was terrified of claiming her voice.

You're on the Vocal Power journey. As I've repeatedly noted, that journey is not outward toward accomplishment. It's not about getting a job as a singer (although that could be a byproduct). Maybe your goal is only to sing "Happy Birthday" at a birthday party and not have you or anyone else flinch. Still, set it aside for now. Apply the empowerment rituals you learned in Chapter 3, and surrender to the process. In the end, it doesn't matter whether you have good "hardware"; if you do not have the commitment and willingness to surrender to the process, the process will be short-circuited.

Singing Is an Emotional Gateway

Vocal Awareness has the ability to open up a deep well of emotions and not everyone is prepared for this experience. However, as with working on poor pitch discrimination, if we allow our emotions to be what they are and stay in the process of the Work—going at our own pace—we can move through, and then beyond difficult emotions. My former student Shoshana Kalisch is a model of such persistence and Self-direction.

Shoshana had read my first book, *The Sound of the Soul*, and mailed me a letter. She was a Holocaust survivor who had taken on the task of traveling the world collecting and performing songs from the Holocaust. But she always felt that there was an emotional element missing when she performed them. Because she was an honest and dedicated person, she knew there was something within herself that she wasn't touching, that she needed to make a more profound connection to the music. She hoped I would be able to help her, flew out from New York City to California, and visited for a couple of days to begin studying.

I asked Shoshana right up front: "Are you sure you want to undertake this?" I knew what the Work would begin to open up within her. Years earlier I had performed the "Erlkönig" by Franz Schubert in concert, a song about a man who is riding in the dead of night with his dying son in his arms. My artistic responsibility required that I be in touch with the truth of that experience. It was painful—perhaps more so because I have two beloved sons—and yet I accessed my wounded feelings and expressed them through the song as honestly and artfully as possible. Now, as Shoshana released her tongue and jaw tension and experienced the aesthetic of the tone, I had her remain cognizant at all times of what was happening technically and emotionally—to work as an *integrated* mind/body/spirit. She was continually monitoring every facet of her Voice. I also had her work from a place of honor of her Deeper Self to make it consciously safe to explore her material.

Shoshana's first visit ended and I didn't hear from her for about six months. When she returned, her Voice had changed markedly. I found out that she had been through a maelstrom of emotions. Nonetheless, she had continued doing her daily vocal sessions, going slowly, like a deep-sea diver decompressing on the way back to the surface. She understood what was happening and was brave enough to take the journey to discover a certain emotional place that she knew existed inside her. Can you see that when we sing with Vocal Awareness, we tap into the meaning and humanity of songs?

Singing can be primal. It's often an easier way than any other to connect with our emotions. Thus, Vocal Awareness is an incredible tool for ongoing Self-discovery. And the more we know about our Selves, the more freedom we have to realize our power.

Three years ago, my student Minnie Lou Guild was vocalizing on a B or B-flat and was struck suddenly by racking sobs that overwhelmed her. She saw images of her father as she had seen him when she was a toddler, and she realized she had never known him. They were estranged in her early childhood. Her emotions came from a nonlogical place that she hadn't anticipated. The pitch and frequency established connections that were moving and profound. Using the Vocal Awareness techniques, she was then able to explore her new inner geography.

It is one thing, for example, to say the words to the folk song "Sometimes I Feel Like a Motherless Child" (*Sometimes I feel like a motherless child—a long way from home*) and quite another to sing this lamentation. Songs tap directly into the central core of the Self, which is the hub of the Voice. When we sing, we breathe life into areas of the psyche that may be rarely accessed. The act of singing opens us emotionally.

Sound is expressed emotion. When we sustain sound as in singing, we sustain emotion.

What's the connection between singing and the rest of our lives? Singing deepens and enriches the awareness of the present moment. It helps us stay connected to our Selves as artists, and we extrapolate lessons that shift the paradigm of our lives. We are sentient beings and this Work helps us be in touch with that. The more we explore the art of singing— the joining of words, melody, and emotion—the more the sound of the voice improves. It has enhanced character and impact. So, when we go on dates, talk to our children or our spouses, if we're in altercations, or have to deal with our bosses or subordinates, we have a more developed instrument at our disposal. Conscious awareness helps us to integrate mind/body/spirit better.

The Spiritual Qualities of Song

Song also has spiritual significance. Modern physics teaches us that sound is vibration, and that vibration is the basis of everything in the universe. Ancient Hindu scriptures say essentially the same thing: "God originally manifests as sound." Sound is the essence, the very core of all nature, a common thread that connects all animate and inanimate life forms. It connects us to everything in the universe at the most infinitesimal levels. Our early ancestors used the power of sound vibration to help attain a sense of attunement with the world around them.

Through the ages, people from all cultures have instinctively used ritualistic song, dance, prayers, and chants to connect with their own center, and to bring that center into resonance with the outer world. From the mesmerizing songs and chants of the shamans of Siberia, Africa, the Americas, and Australia, to the chanting rabbis, priests, and monks of Judaism, Christianity, Islam, Hinduism, and Buddhism, sound has been our primary means of resonating with the sacred inside and outside ourselves. A shaman intones a chant to bring on a mystical trance that recaptures the original experience of unity. A solitary yogi repeats the sacred syllable *Om* in a Himalayan cave. A Navajo medicine man dances and sings in a healing ceremony. Tibetan monks chant in unison in a remote monastery. Roman Catholic priests sing Gregorian chants.

The longer you use the Vocal Awareness method, the clearer the spiritual element of the mind/body/spirit integration will become for you. When we find freedom and joy in song, it is as though energy is moving through us. The rituals of *Pay Attention/Deeper Listening* and *Take My Time* enable us to tap into and have the pleasure of this sensation.

Vocal Awareness Differs from Other Kinds of Singing Lessons

As singing teachers, many of us think we have all the answers, even when we don't. And our students often give over their power to us because they feel an almost mystical awe about singing. Unlike dancing, writing, painting, or playing an instrument, singing is a far more intangible experience. We cannot see one's voice. It's also a transient moment-to-moment experience. Just as in life, we truly never know exactly what's going to happen next. This feels risky and scares us. (Once again, the metaphor.) I often think of classical singers as bullfighters wondering, "Am I going to hit the high note tonight or am I going to be gored?" The important point is that on stage they confront it. In Vocal Power, we want to do the same thing not only on stage but also in life.

When we are singing, we want to soar and push the envelope, but we need to have the abilities and refinements that back up the experience. We have to follow the rules. Otherwise, like Icarus in the ancient Greek myth, we're going to fly too close to the sun.

The feathers of his wings were held together by wax and melted; thus, he fell to his death. His father, Daedalus, had taught him the rules, but Icarus thought he knew better and so went against the instruction. I want you to follow the rules and use the Vocal Awareness techniques, so you can soar consciously and without fear.

I usually scribble notes in the margins of my programs at classical vocal concerts. Even when the performers are professionals, I often find that they have too much tongue tension, a little bit of spreading in the mouth, and shallow unconscious breathing. None of these flaws are startling, yet I believe that these details have relegated many singers to second tier status throughout their careers. These minor details may have affected every area of their lives from their income, to where they reside, to whether they travel, to whom they know, as well as to their professional accomplishments and personal fulfillment. This relates to the issue of timing, talent, and tenacity that we discussed in the last chapter. These artists may have wonderful vocal instruments, but their technique lets them down when they need it most.

In typical singing lessons, teachers have their students do scales mechanically—rather like jumping jacks. This is not necessarily the most creative and artistic experience. It may develop the voice, but not artistically, aesthetically, or spiritually. Don't get me wrong: Scales are important. But it is not only what we do, rather *how* we do what we do that matters. When we do scales, we need to be meticulous and apply our rituals consciously. There is much more Vocal Power in sending the vocal energy through the Nasal Edge and Arc of Sound and utilizing all the other rituals on the Vocal Awareness Checklist. There is more to be gained by meticulous attention to detail and *Deeper Listening.* "Perfect" technique doesn't interest me in the slightest. I care passionately, however, about *maximizing* expression. It just so happens that to have maximal expression, you must have maximal technique. Therefore, technique is only a means to an end, not an end in itself. The way my client Carina works is a good example of this.

I met Carina in a rehearsal studio where she was singing songs that a mutual friend had composed. We began working together soon after. Her voice was already intrinsically beautiful. She had sung all her life. As we began the Work, I realized that I rarely had a student who trusted me fully in the first lesson as she did. The results were stunning for both of us. She made breakthrough after breakthrough by spending 45 minutes on six bars of music using Vocal Awareness. Two years later, we finished recording her own album of songs in Spanish—she's Mexican-Basque by heritage.

Notwithstanding the fact that I've always found her generous and courageous, she made another breakthrough a year after that. She finally gave herself permission to sing for the sheer pleasure of it—in other words, for her Self. In the process, she discovered a great bounty for her and for those in her presence as she sings. As the poet Percy Bysshe Shelley once wrote, "I want to sing like birds sing, not worrying who hears and what they think." Today, Carina's Voice sounds freer, warmer, and more emotional than ever—and her expression is much more intimate and personally revealing.

THE VOCAL AWARENESS SINGING WORKOUT

Now, we're going to build on the foundation of the Vocal Awareness workout you learned in Chapter 4. Once again, you'll need to have the Vocal Awareness Checklist nearby, within eyeshot (see below). And you'll need to gather the same tools: a mirror, a washcloth or handkerchief, a pencil, and a tape recorder or video camera (both optional). Remember: Always, always, always begin by standing or sitting in stature.

The Vocal Awareness Checklist

1. Thank You to My Source;
2. Love and Let Go;
3. Allow a Silent, Loving, Down-through-my-body Breath;
4. See the Nasal Edge and Arc of Sound;
5. Pay Attention/Deeper Listening;
6. Take My Time;
7. Be Conscious of Self.

Musical accompaniment is optional for the first and second aspects of the singing workout. I often prefer to vocalize *a capella*. This gives me the freedom to control my own tempo, or pace. Otherwise, the tempo would be dictated by accompaniment. Being in control of the tempo affords me a greater opportunity to focus on my feelings. Accompaniment has different benefits. It can help me feel more "musical." That's why it is essential for the third aspect of the singing workout.

For the aspects where you decide to use musical accompaniment, I recommend using recorded accompaniments, producing a tape-recording with which you can sing along. If you do not play the piano, flute, or another instrument yourself, you may locate an accompanist for hire at your local house of worship, a junior college, a music school, or in the telephone book.

Once you have found an accompanist, first, ask that person to record the notes for the exercises in the Singing Warm-Up in your best key. Then ask them to record the songs you want to sing for the Bridge and the Performance aspects, also in your best key. Have them create two versions of the music. The first version should be relatively slow and emphasize the melody line that you'll be singing. The second version can be in tempo—up to speed—and more elaborately fleshed out.

Instead of using an accompanist to record songs for the Bridge and Performance aspects of the Singing Workout, or in addition to using one, you may also practice singing along with karaoke tapes. Be aware, however, that these may not be in your best key. Take extra special care, therefore, not to strain your voice.

You can do the singing workout on its own, or you can do it at the end of your daily vocal workout. Make sure to practice it everyday. Singing has validity for its own sake, but you'll notice that it also enhances the speaking voice.

The First Aspect: The Singing Warm-Up

In the Singing Warm-Up, you're going to use exercises similar to those you did in the spoken Warm-Up in Chapter 4, building on the Yawn-Sigh.

Warm-Up 1: The Musical Yawn-Sigh

Begin by standing or sitting in stature. As you learned before, make a "V" with one hand and place it on your chin and jaw. Apply a gentle, downward pressure to ease your jaw open. Your mouth should be open to a length of about three fingers. Allow your tongue to rest against your bottom teeth. Keep your head level—you don't want it to drop forward as your jaw is released. Check your mirror to see that you're doing the technique correctly.

Now, place two fingers under your tongue—not too far back—allowing it to release forward on top of your fingers. Use your thumb of the same hand to press gently under your chin at the spot where you can feel the base of the tongue muscle in order to check for tension.

Each time you do one of these singing exercises, I want you to remember to use an aspirated "H" sound (see p. 102 in Chapter 4). "H" initiates vibrations in the vocal folds, which allows air to pass through them. I also want you to hold your first note for a moment. Don't drift off or descend through your note. This moment enables you to build focus and momentum. It reminds me of a toy car I had when I was a child. It operated by friction. I would roll the wheels in place, and then the moment I released it, it shot off across the floor. We're doing the same thing here. We're building energy in the voice and giving ourselves time to coordinate the mind/body/spirit.

Then, starting on a note that feels comfortable, sing the sound *Yaw* in one continuous slide down a full octave while *seeing the Arc*. Don't let the energy "drop."

y___a___a___a___a___a___a___w

Next, sing the same descending octave, using the sound *Hee*.

h___e___e___e___e___e___e

Now place your hand in the Nasal Edge position, and, seeing the Arc of Sound, sing, *Yaw* five times, going one step down the scale each time. Stop in the middle if necessary to *Allow a Silent, Loving, Down-through-my-body Breath*, and then begin again on the same note you sang just before stopping.

y_____a___a___a_____w

Be sure to glide ever so slowly from one note to the next, *always subtly energizing the voice before moving to the next note,* also slightly crescendo. This enables you to use the natural support of the abdominal muscles more effectively. I call this slurring connection between the notes the *plié,* or the elevator technique. When you *plié,* you go down to go up. When an elevator goes down, the weight and pulleys go up—and vice versa. We use this technique so that we'll always be energizing the voice, not stopping and starting and leaving pieces of ourselves behind and disconnecting note from note. The *plié* helps us to keep momentum rolling.

Remove your hand and repeat the last portion of the exercise simply visualizing the Nasal Edge and Arc of Sound.

Repeat, starting your scale half a note higher and then half a note lower.

Singing Warm-Up 2: The Staccato Pattern Scale

Staccato is the Italian word for short and sharp. In this exercise, you will be inserting the index and middle fingers of one hand beneath your tongue as you do the Yawn-Sigh, and you'll use the sounds: *What, Hi, Haw, Hi, Haw.* When I do the staccato pattern scale, I always imagine a basketball player shooting free throws. The *attack* should have the same emphasis each time; you're aiming for the same mark. There's always a sense of "lift and come down."

Begin by standing or sitting in stature. As you learned before, make a "V" with one hand and place it on your chin and jaw. Apply a gentle, downward pressure to ease your jaw open. Your mouth should be open to a length of about three fingers. Allow your tongue to rest gently against your bottom teeth. Keep your head level—you don't want it to drop forward as your jaw is released. Check your mirror to see that you're doing the technique correctly.

Now, place two fingers under your tongue—not too far back—allowing it to release forward on top of your fingers. Use your thumb of the same hand to press gently under your chin at the spot where you can feel the base of the tongue muscle in order to check for tension.

Now, sing *What, Hi, Haw, Hi, Haw* (using the notes below), holding the last *Haw* to finish.

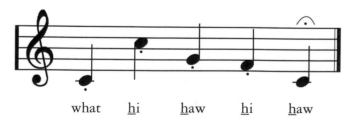

what   hi   haw   hi   haw

Then, go through the same sounds while using your washcloth or handkerchief to perform the Tongue Pull.

Finally, sing the same sounds while using the Pencil Technique.

The Second Aspect: The Singing Bridge

Songs contain two life forms, lyrics and music, which were created separately. So, in the Singing Bridge, we work individually on both elements starting with the lyrics. For the purpose of teaching, we'll be using the music and lyrics from two traditional songs: "The Riddle Song" and "He's Got The Whole World In His Hands." I chose "The Riddle Song" for its simple and poignant melody and lyric and "He's Got the Whole World in His Hands" for its passionate, fervent, and joyous expression.

Begin by writing the lyrics down on a separate sheet of paper. This will help you identify with the lyrics as a story rather than with the hyphens and bar lines that surround them. Work on the lyrics as you would any other text by applying the Tongue Pull, the Two-Finger Yawn-Sigh, and the Pencil Technique, as you learned in Chapter 4. Go back and review those Bridge techniques if necessary (see p. 118).

It would sound like this for "The Riddle Song":

🎵 *I gave my love a cherry that had no stone,*
(Tongue Pull)

🎵 *I gave my love a chicken that had no bone,*
(Two-Fingers)

🎵 *I told my love a story that had no end,*
(Pencil Technique)

🎵 *I gave my love a baby that's no cryin.*
(Sing naturally)

It would sound like this for "He's Got The Whole World In His Hands":

🎵 *He's got the whole world in His hands,*
(Tongue Pull)

🎵 *He's got the whole wide world in His hands,*
(Two Fingers)

🎵 *He's got the whole world in His hands,*
(Pencil Technique)

🎵 *He's got the whole world in His hands.*
(Sing naturally)

Please feel free to apply this structure to all verses.

Always stand or sit in stature before you begin. Apply the rituals on the Vocal Awareness Checklist—you can write notes as reminders about these in the margins of the song. Speak very nasally.

See the Nasal Edge and Arc of Sound. And remember to take your time.

At some point, ask yourself some questions about the meaning of the story you're singing and your identity, so you can create a subtext for your performance. You never have to reveal your answers to anyone. They can be secret. Investigate:

♪ Who am I?

♪ Where am I?

♪ Why?

♪ What motivates me to sing this song?

After working on the lyrics, you'll work on the melody line of your song. Begin by humming these songs keeping the lips *gently* together—no tension—but maintain the nasal edge. Do this—hum *a capella* very slowly. Remember the *plié.* Stand or sit in stature. Apply the rituals. Stop and breathe as often as you need. Review the principles you used in the Warm-Up. Remember: Don't leave pieces out.

Next, using the sound of *Hah* as in "hat," do the following:

NOTE: Sustain the *Hah* gently, nasally. Do not attack each note separately.

He's Got the Whole World In His Hands

With spirit.

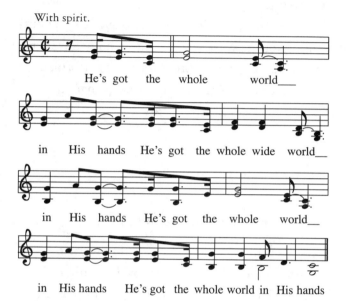

He's got the whole world___ in His hands He's got the whole wide world___ in His hands He's got the whole world__ in His hands He's got the whole world in His hands

2. He's got the montains and the rivers in His hands
   He's got the montains and the rivers in His hands
   He's got the montains and the rivers in His hands
   He's got the wide world in His hands

(Chorus)

3. He's got the mighty and the humble in His hands
   He's got the mighty and the humble in His hands
   He's got the mighty and the humble in His hands
   He's got the wide world in His hands

(Chorus)

4. He's got the kingdom up in Heaven in His hands
   He's got the kingdom up in Heaven in His hands
   He's got the kingdom up in Heaven in His hands
   He's got the wide world in His hands

The Riddle Song

Sing sweetly and lovingly.

I gave my love a cher-ry that had no stone; I gave my love a chick-en that had no bone. I told my love a sto-ry that had no end; I gave my love a ba-by that's no cry-in!

How can there be a cherry
　　that has no stone?
How can there be a chicken
　　that has no bone?
How can there be a story
　　that has no end?
How can there be a baby
　　that's no crying?

A cherry when it's blooming,
　　it has no stone,
A chicken when it's pippin',
　　it has no bone,
The story that I love you,
　　it has no end,
A baby when it's sleeping,
　　it's no crying.

Tongue Pull, The Two-Finger Yawn-Sigh, Using the Pencil Technique.

Always remember to do the Work expressively and sensually.

Singing Freely: First humming. Second *Hah*.

Always remember to keep the pressure flow constant, your support pulling up and through the musical line, and the tongue and jaw releasing tension.

Optional: Record your impressions in your Vocal Power journal.

The Third Aspect: The Singing Performance

Now we come to the third aspect, which is to sing the song and feel the joy of singing. This is your opportunity to put together all the work you've done so far.

Begin by standing or sitting in stature. Check your mirror. Visualize the Vocal Awareness Checklist, and then sing first the "The Riddle Song." Allow your Self to sing freely, confidently, and consciously. When you feel ready, apply the same principles and enjoy "He's Got the Whole World In His Hands."

Optional: Record your impressions in your Vocal Power journal.

The unknown is the last thrill ride.

Terry Iacuso

Apply these techniques to all your favorite songs. The bottom line is to enhance the joy of singing and your personal sovereignty.

Guidelines for Singing Lessons

If you decide to take singing lessons, seek out a teacher who is a member of the National Association of Teachers of Singing. This is not an absolute guarantee that the teacher will be good; however, it does indicate a certain degree of professionalism. To further evaluate your singing teacher, apply the following four guidelines:

- ♪ You must feel emotionally safe during your lessons.
- ♪ You must be allowed to record your lessons.
- ♪ You must be allowed to ask questions.

♪ You should be physically well when leaving your lesson—your larynx or throat should not hurt.

Singing can be such an intimate experience that any teacher with whom you work is privileged to participate in the birth of your Voice. So use your powers of discernment when you select a teacher, and do not be afraid to switch if you feel disrespected.

Singing Is for Everyone

What better way to reclaim your Voice than by raising it joyfully in song! Sing around the house. Sing with your children. Have you ever seen an inhibited three-year-old? It's virtually an oxymoron. Are three-year-olds afraid to sing? No, of course not. Singing is so natural. My student Carina's daughter, Ciela, has been a part of our lessons since she was in her mother's womb. At six months, I sang to her often, saying, "Watch my lips, Ciela." At nine months, she began to vocalize—in tune. That's how intrinsic the ability to sing is. Now at two and a half years, she can sing many songs in tune and has also recorded a brief duet with her mother of the Spanish lullaby "Las Mañanitas" on Carina's album.

Give yourself permission to sing. Singing is your birthright. Join a local church, temple, or community choir. Many nonprofessional singers begin their career in the local choir and continue in choirs after they become professional. Many other nonprofessional singers find their fulfillment singing in the shower. *Singing is for everyone.*

Going Deeper—
Breathing into …

I'm closing my book with some of my favorite
thoughts, poems, and parables. I am sharing them
with you for two reasons: First, because they have come
to mean a lot to me in my work—they can help provide
an inspirational "due north" when you need a moment
of personal enlightenment. And second, the intimate
and meaningful pieces will allow you to integrate more
deliberately your Vocal Power technique with a rich
tapestry of language. Through the integration of the
Three Aspects, you will have the opportunity to experience the impact of Vocal Power at a cellular level
through the consciousness of a loving breath and
through the implementation of the Edge and the Arc.
Please allow yourself to feel the spiritual and vibrational
resonance move you and move through you. With these
words and thoughts, you will have the opportunity to
experience a profound change. Don't just read them and
enjoy them in the usual way, experience them deeply.

Be still and know that I am God.
Be still and know that I am.
Be still and know.
Be still.
Be.

Ps. 46:10

♪ ♪ ♪

{My light} is most precious not only to me, but above all to
the darkness of the creator. He needs man to illuminate his
creation.

—C. G. Jung

♪ ♪ ♪

I sing to my soul a song of life. I sing to my soul a song of
love. I sing to my soul to sing who I am. I sing to my soul.

—Arthur Joseph

(I created this at the Esalen Institute a few years ago
and we sang it as a descant.)

Had I the Heavens' embroidered cloths,
Enwrought with golden and silver light,
The blue and the dim and the dark cloths
Of night and light and the half-light,
I would spread the cloths under your feet:
But I, being poor, have only my dreams,
I have spread my dreams under your feet;
Tread softly because you tread on my dreams.

—W. B. Yeats

♪ ♪ ♪

Creativity, as usually understood, needs not only a what,
a talent, but a "who"—strong personal characteristics, a
strong identity, personal sensibility, a personal style, which
flow into the talent, interfuse it, give it a personal body and
form. Creativity in this sense involves the power to originate,
to break away from the existing ways of looking at things,
to move freely in the realm of the imagination, to create and
recreate worlds fully in one's mind—while supervising all
this with a critical inner eye. Creativity has to do with
inner life, with the flow of new ideas and strong feelings.

—Dr. Oliver Sacks

Word to the Wise

Nothing in the world can take the place of persistence.
Talent will not; nothing is more common than unsuccessful
men with talent.
Genius will not; unrewarded genius is almost a proverb.
Education will not; the world is full of educated derelicts.
Persistence and determination alone are omnipotent.

—President Calvin Coolidge

♪ ♪ ♪

I long to accomplish a great and noble task, but it is my
chief duty to accomplish small tasks as if they were great
and noble.

—Helen Keller

♪ ♪ ♪

I looked where no one could see.
And I saw what no one else saw.
What no one was meant to see!
When all's said and done;
It's a mean world!
I'd never want to be human.
But for the fact;
That it's the thing to be!

—"The Shadow" by Hans Christian Andersen, 1847

Destiny is not a matter of chance, it's a matter of choice.
It is not a thing to be waited for, it is a thing to be achieved.

—William Jennings Bryan

♪ ♪ ♪

To acknowledge your truth is not arrogant.
To not acknowledge it is!

—Arthur Joseph

♪ ♪ ♪

We must be still and still moving into another intensity,
for a further union, a deeper communion.

—T. S. Eliot

♪ ♪ ♪

My first book closed with a poem by the nobel laureate Seamus Heaney called "Personal Helicon." I closed my book with it because the last stanza of the poem explained why I created this work.

Now, to pry into roots, to finger slime, to stare, big-eyed Narcissus, into some spring is beneath all adult dignity. I rhyme to see myself, to set the darkness echoing.

Why am I afraid to dance, I who love music,
rhythm and song?
Why am I afraid to live, I who love life and the living
colors of earth and sky and sea?
Why am I afraid to believe, I who admire commitment,
sincerity, and trust?

Why am I afraid of love? I who yearn to give myself in love?
Why am I afraid, I who am not afraid?
Why must I be so ashamed of my strength, or of my weakness?
Why must I live in a cage like a criminal, defying, and
hating, I who love peace and friendship?
Was I born without a skin, that I must wear armor in
order to touch or to be touched?

—Eugene O'Neill

♪ ♪ ♪

There is a vitality, a life force, a quickening that is trans-
lated through you into action, and because there is only one
of you in all time, this expression is unique. And if you
block it, it will never exist through any other medium and
be lost. The world will not have it.

It is not your business to determine how good it is, nor how
valuable it is, nor how it compares with other expressions. It
is your business to keep it yours clearly and directly, to keep
the channel open. You do not even have to believe in yourself
or your work. You have to keep open and aware directly to
the urges that motivate you. Keep the channel open.

—Martha Graham to Agnes DeMille

*Until one is committed, there is
hesitancy, the chance to draw back;
always, ineffectiveness concerning all
acts of initiative (and creation)
There is one elementary truth, the
ignorance of which kills countless ideas
and splendid plans:
that the moment one definitely
commits oneself, then Providence
moves too.
All sorts of things occur to help one that would
 never otherwise have occurred.
A whole stream of events issues from
the decision, raising in one's favour all
manner of unforeseen incidents and
meetings and material assistance
which no one could have dreamed
would have come their way . . .
Whatever you can do or dream you can,
begin it. Boldness has genius, power
and magic in it.
Begin it now.*

—W. H. Murray/Goethe

Desiderata

Go placidly amid the noise and haste
and remember what peace there may be in silence.
As far as possible without surrender, be on good terms
    with all persons.
Speak your truth quietly and clearly and listen to others,
even the dull and ignorant; they too have their story.
Avoid loud and aggressive persons; they are vexatious
    to the spirit.
If you compare yourself with others you may become
    vain or bitter,
for always there will be greater and lesser persons
    than yourself.
Enjoy your achievements as well as your plans.
Keep interested in your career, however humble;
it is a real possession in the changing fortunes of time.
Exercise caution in your business affairs,
for the world is full of trickery.
But let this not blind you to what virtue there is.
Many persons strive for high ideals
and everywhere life is full of heroism.
Be yourself.
Especially do not feign affection.
Neither be cynical about love,
for in the face of all aridity and disappointment
it is as perennial as the grass.

Take kindly the counsel of the years,
gracefully surrendering the things of youth.
Nurture strength of spirit to shield you in sudden misfortune.
But do not distress yourself with imaginings.
Many fears are born of fatigue and loneliness.
Beyond a wholesome discipline be gentle with yourself.
You are a child of the universe no less than the trees
    and the stars.
You have a right to be here.
And whether it is clear to you or not,
no doubt the universe is unfolding as it should.
Therefore be at peace with God,
whatever you conceive him to be,
and whatever your labours and aspirations in the noisy
    confusion of life,
keep peace with your soul.
With all its sham and drudgery and broken dreams
it is still a beautiful world.
Be cheerful. Strive to be happy.

> —Max Ehrman, 1927. Found on a wall of Old Saint
> Paul's Church, Baltimore, Maryland.

*If for a moment God were to forget that I am a rag doll
and granted me a piece of life, I probably wouldn't say
everything that I think; rather, I would think about
everything that I say.*

*I would value things, not of their worth but for what
they mean.*

*I would sleep less, dream more, understanding that for each
minute we close our eyes, we lose sixty seconds of light.*

*I would walk when others hold back, I would wake when
others sleep, I would listen when others talk.*

And how I would enjoy a good chocolate ice-cream!

*If God were to give me a piece of life, I would dress simply,
throw myself face first into the sun, baring not only my
body but also my soul.*

*My God, if I had a heart, I would write my hate on ice,
and wait for the sun to show.*

*Over the stars I would paint with a Van Gogh dream a
Benedetti poem, and a Serrat song would be the sere-
nade I'd offer to the moon.*

*I would water roses with my tears, to feel the pain of their
thorns and the red kiss of their petals . . .*

*My God, if I had a piece of life . . . I wouldn't let a single
day pass without telling the people I love that I love them.*

*I would convince each woman and each man that they are
my favorites, and I would live in love with love.*

*I would show men how very wrong they are to think that
they cease to be in love, when they grow old, not knowing
that they grow old when they cease to be in love!*

To a child I shall give wings, but I shall let him learn to
fly on his own.
I would teach the old that death does not come with old age,
but with forgetting.
So much have I learned from you, oh men . . .
I have learned that everyone wants to live at the top of the
mountain, without knowing that real happiness is in
how it is scaled.
I have learned that when a newborn child first squeezes his
father's finger in his tiny fist, he has him trapped
forever.
I have learned that a man has the right to look down on
another only when he has to help the other get to his feet.
From you I have learned so many things, but in truth they
won't be of much use, for when I keep them within this
suitcase, unhappily shall I be dying.

—Gabriel Garcia Marquez, 2000

(This beautiful story was sent to me in a Christmas letter
received in 2002 by my friend, Dann Moss.)

♪ ♪ ♪

I want to unfold. I don't want to stay folded anywhere.
Because where I am folded, there I am a lie.

—Rainer Maria Rilke,
translated by Robert Bly from "I Am Too Alone"

The following are translations by Anita Barrows and Joanna Macy from Rilke's "Book of Hours":

Lösch mir die Augen aus: ich kann dich sehn
Extinguish my eyes, I'll go on seeing you
Seal my ears, I'll go on hearing you
and without feet I can make my way to you
without a mouth I can swear your name.

Break off my arms, I'll take hold of you
with my heart as with a hand
Stop my heart, and my brain will start to beat
And if you consume my brain with fire
I'll feel you burn in every drop of my blood.

Vielleicht, daß ich durch schwere Berge gehe
It feels as though I make my way
through massive rock
like a vein of ore
alone, encased.

I am so deep inside it
I can't see the path or any distance:
everything is close
and everything closing in on me
has turned to stone.

Since I still don't know enough about pain,
this terrible darkness makes me small.
If it's you, though—
press down hard on me, break in
that I may know the weight of your hand,
and you, the fullness of my cry.

Ich glaube an Alles noch nie Gesagte
I believe in all that has never yet been spoken
I want to free what waits within me
so that what no one has dared to wish for
may for once spring clear
without my contriving.

If this is arrogant, God, forgive me,
but this is what I need to say.
May what I do flow from me like a river,
no forcing and no holding back,
the way it is with children.

Then in these swelling and ebbing currents,
these deepening tides moving out, returning,
I will sing you as no one ever has,
streaming through widening channels
into the open sea.

Epilogue

*I dream in my dream all the dreams of the other
dreamers, and I become the other dreamers.*

--Walt Whitman

Some 30 years ago, as I was preparing to go to bed,
a thought occurred to me while I was reading a
magazine. I didn't want to get up and write it down,
but the thought wouldn't leave. So I was forced to get
up, find a pen, and write it down, which I did in the
margin of the magazine. The thought was this:

> Voice is the only artistic experience that is both
> finite and infinite at the same time. It is fallible and
> fragile, gone in an instant, unseen, only felt—
> remembered from the past even a long moment ago,
> anticipated, sensing its future, even as its present is
> just occurring. It is temporal, visceral, organic—such
> a complex, simple, and beguiling state.

A few years later, I was invited to the Institute for
the Advanced Studies of the Communication Processes
at the University of Florida. While working there for
a couple of weeks, I spoke with two of the greatest
voice scientists in the world about this principle that

had come through to me so clearly and completely. They loved it. They believed it. During the visit, one more thought came to me—that I could substitute the words "life" or "love" for the word "voice" and achieve the same paradigmatic model.

Life is the only artistic experience that is both finite and infinite at the same time . . .

Love is fallible and fragile, gone in an instant, unseen, only felt . . .

With this new insight, my understanding of my work deepened and the puzzle was complete. Vocal Awareness teaches about the trinity of life as much as it teaches about the trinity of mind/body/spirit. Vocal Awareness is the integration of life/love/voice—all synonyms for the same thing. The metaphor was now crystal clear: *You are your Voice, and your Voice is you.*

As you have been reading this book, exploring the rituals, vocal techniques, and activities contained within it, you have no doubt begun to sense the remarkable life-altering potential of the Vocal Awareness method. I'm sure that you can already hear and feel a difference in the sound of your voice—and also hear and feel a difference in the "sound" of your inner voice. As you continue showing up and doing the Work on a regular basis, please remember that the only reason for doing it is to bring your Self joy, sovereignty, and personal empowerment—the symbols of Vocal Power.

The Vocal Awareness method offers a metaphorical, spiritual, and practical structure upon which you can build a life of honor and success in *your* way and with *your* power. It can be a bulwark against the changing tides of life. But you have to be specific and compassionate and actually apply the tenets of the System in order to experience its benefits. Long ago, I realized that there are no shortcuts in life. It is not enough just to have read this book. You have to participate in the Work everyday. Whether you choose to implement this information is your decision. I hope you will. Its principles are my vocation and my lifelong artistic and professional passion. I would love that you enjoy similar rewards and enthusiasm.

Since you have come this far, you've already experienced meaningful success. But please recognize that your Vocal Power journey is just beginning. And please do not assume that you've mastered Vocal Awareness because you have come so far on your journey. In fact, it is a lifelong process. Allow for the possibility that the journey doesn't have to be arduous, filled with brutal challenges and obstacles. Keep in mind that it can be an exhilarating adventure in the company of a wise and loving guide—*you, applying Vocal Awareness to achieve Vocal Power!*

So, my friend (and I hope by this time that you feel as though we have become friends, because we both have shared a lot through these pages), complete the book and then put it aside. You are entering a new chapter of your life. When necessary, return to it as you would return to a quiet corner for solace, or to a dear teacher for inspiration and guidance. Continue your ascent. Continue soaring. And strive to take the journey inward as well. *Feel the full investiture of your Self in every breath, in every sound, and with the fullest integration of mind/body/spirit.*

Thank you for your trust. Thank you for sharing your Self.

About the Author

The *Vocal Workout* was originated by Arthur Joseph almost four decades ago. The Vocal Awareness System integrates your mind/body/spirit.

Arthur Joseph has taught Vocal Awareness in European palaces, Ivy League universities and renowned institutions. CEOs for *Fortune* 500 companies, politicians, and college students all seek him out. Movie stars, TV stars, stage performers, broadcasters, sports celebrities, and professional singers consider him their secret weapon. Schoolteachers, lawyers, therapists, and doctors have all known success through Vocal Awareness.

Arthur resides with his family in Los Angeles, California.

For additional information, songs, and other support materials, please visit us on the Web at w w w.vocalawareness.com.